For a complete list of Management Books 2000 titles,
visit our web-site on www.mb2000.com

The original idea for the 'In Ninety Minutes' series was
presented to the publishers by Graham Willmott, author
of 'Forget Debt in Ninety Minutes'. Thanks are due to
him for suggesting what has become a major series to
help business people, entrepreneurs, managers,
supervisors and others to greatly improve their personal
performance, after just a short period of study.

Other titles in the 'in Ninety Minutes' series are:

Forget Debt in 90 Minutes
Understand Accounts in 90 Minutes
Working Together in 90 Minutes
25 Management Techniques in 90 Minutes
Supply Chain in 90 Minutes
Practical Negotiating in 90 Minutes
Find That Job in 90 Minutes
Budgeting in 90 Minutes
Telling People in 90 Minutes
Faster Promotion in 90 Minutes
Networking in 90 Minutes
Payroll in 90 Minutes
... other titles will be added

The series editor is James Alexander

Submissions of possible titles for this series or for management books in
general will be welcome. MB2000 are always keen to discuss possible new
works that might be added to their extensive list of books for people who
mean business.

The ultimate guide to marketing yourself

PERFECT CVs in 90 Minutes

Frank Thaxton

2000

First published in 2005 by Management Books 2000 Ltd
Forge House, Limes Road
Kemble, Cirencester
Gloucestershire, GL7 6AD, UK
Tel: 0044 (0) 1285 771441
Fax: 0044 (0) 1285 771055
E-mail: info@mb2000.com
Web: www.mb2000.com

Printed and bound in Great Britain by Digital Books Logistics Ltd of Peterborough

British Library Cataloguing in Publication Data is available

ISBN 1-85252-499-5

Contents

About the author

Frank Thaxton has a manufacturing, finance and venture capital background and has run his own consultancy business since 1985. Over the last 15 years he has focussed on coaching people in their careers and on starting new careers, and has advised on setting up, or buying into, independent business. Clients have ranged from school and college leavers to main board directors of listed PLCs. He has covered the whole range of careers advice with clients as they move from one role to another, returning to work with him for subsequent career moves. The review of CVs was part of his life for many years as a senior manager/recruiter in business, and since 1989 he has advised hundreds of clients on how to write a good CV – clients who have then been successful in using their CVs to find satisfying new jobs.

His book *'Stop Dreaming and Start Doing'* on how to start a business in the United Kingdom is also published by Management Books 2000 Ltd and he recently finished a similar book geared to the Australian market.

Acknowledgements

One thing I have learned is that nearly everyone has a view on what an ideal CV should look like – and often the views are conflicting! I've benefited from much advice, whether from professional colleagues or people I have met briefly at barbecues etc – all of whom have shown no reluctance at all in giving their views. I'm grateful to all – it's been most valuable. I would however especially like to thank Ron Owen and Julia Thaxton for their assistance and advice in putting this book together – their help has been much appreciated.

If you have any comments or suggestions for improvements in the next edition, please send them to me at the publishers info@mb2000.com, or at frankthaxton@tvpl.co.uk

1

Introduction

You spot an interesting job advertisement or a head-hunter rings you and says, 'Could you send me a resumé/CV?'

Isn't that really the time when we start thinking about writing or updating our CV? And we react by saying to ourselves, 'I really must put together/revise my CV quickly and send it off' – probably with some regret that we didn't do it much earlier. Most of us don't plan ahead for preparing and revising a CV – it's a last minute scramble!

We haven't much time before it's needed, so it's a rush job, under time pressure, with little chance to review etc. But we say to ourselves 'That's okay, it'll do.' What we are often doing when we adopt this approach is under-selling ourselves, not giving ourselves the opportunities we deserve and for which we have worked so hard. We're almost planning to fail.

Think of it in general business terms. If you were selling a product – any product – what would the boss say to you in reply to your comment, 'That's okay, it'll do'? If you were selling any product, whether new or existing, a lot of effort would go into the marketing of it – researching the market, looking at why people buy, what they are looking for, how to package the product or service and so on. You may have come across this marketing preparation in previous jobs or in your business studies. Teams of people work for weeks on end to produce marketing literature to promote the product or service, and to invite potential purchasers to contact the seller. Only when the marketing is done effectively is there a chance to sell. In a competitive marketplace, your marketing literature has to be good.

Junk mail

Often, when marketing literature is sent out by direct mail, it ends up as 'junk mail' – which is what we call the mail that is specifically targeted at and sent to us, but which we find insufficiently interesting to read when we receive it. Why do we think that? Often, because it seems to us as the reader that it is poorly presented, inadequately prepared, and irrelevant for us. It doesn't 'hit our hot buttons' or whatever your particular phrase is. We can't be bothered to follow-up the initial marketing literature sent by the seller to find out if the product or service is relevant or valuable to us – we'd much rather bin it. As such, we may be missing a golden opportunity to find something we really want and could use – but we don't follow it up because the poor marketing materials do not attract our attention or impress us sufficiently.

Junk CVs?

With CVs, I think it's a very similar situation. When you send out your CV, you are starting the marketing process for a fairly expensive product/service. If the 'purchaser' were to add up the cost of employing you (salary, on-costs of the benefits package, costs of work-space etc) the cost is quite high – and it's on an annual basis too; it's not just a once-off purchase. And then there's the damage you could do to the company or business if the recruiter or manager gets it wrong. All of which adds up to a fairly expensive 'service' that you are trying to sell. Your CV is the material that you send out to market this expensive package. Will you easily accept it being binned as 'junk mail' ('poorly presented, inadequately prepared, and irrelevant') just because you haven't taken time over it, assessed the market requirements and so on. If you do, you will almost certainly miss opportunities to sell yourself.

What this book will do is provide you with some guidelines for writing a relevant CV, one that starts to market you persuasively and one that will help you through the door to start the process of selling yourself. Your CV has got to be good – firstly because you are – but also because you are usually competing with many others seeking to influence the same 'purchaser'. Your CV must be relevant and persuasive, because you are up against many other 'products' in the market – few people ask for and receive just one CV; yours is likely to be one of perhaps several hundred initially received for the same advertised position. By reading through the subsequent chapters of this book and following the relevant guidance, you will produce a much better CV to market your services. You want opportunities to sell yourself – an excellent product – and so you need and deserve excellent marketing literature.

I said 'relevant guidance' because I believe that there is no such thing as one perfect CV suitable for everyone. There is such a thing as a brilliant or dazzling CV for you – but you will have to make some choices in its preparation. I'll guide you through those choices and help you to produce a dazzling CV! It will only take about 90 minutes to read the book and I've summarised the advice in Chapter 13 and given some examples in Appendix I. One thing is for sure, we all need advice; in my entire career as a coach, I've never met anyone whose CV couldn't be improved – sometimes radically.

At the end of each chapter, I've included some 'Key Points' to remember from it, together with some space for you to add your own learning points

Note:

Where I have used the masculine pronoun ('he', him, or 'his') it is not because most people writing CVs are male, but because any other approach seems to me to become either cumbersome or sounds affected.

I've also chosen generally to use the description 'CV' rather than curriculum vitae, resumé, career summary, career history, employment history, list of positions/jobs held, personal profile or any other name. I'm sure there are more descriptions for the document outlining your career to date. I've just called it a CV!

2

What is a CV?

2.1 – Introduction

Let's start by thinking about what a CV is. People generally prepare a CV summarising their career to date, listing the organisations worked for, the jobs held and so on. Does something like this do the job? To answer that question, we have to consider the purpose of a CV and then produce a document that stands the best chance of achieving that purpose. In this chapter, we'll look at the real purpose of a CV so that we can meet the implicit needs.

2.2 – The purpose of a CV

What is the purpose of a CV? I can almost hear you saying 'That's easy; I want to provide an accurate, honest and complete summary of my career to date.' **Absolutely not!** Yes it must be honest, but I believe your major purpose in sending out your CV is to *excite and interest the reader* and create the need to meet you. How do you do that? By understanding the various purposes of the CV and then preparing a CV to meet them. The resultant CV may then achieve its purpose – when both you and the reader will see it as a brilliant CV. So, what are the purposes of a CV?

The first and over-riding purpose of a CV is to be a personal marketing document. You are marketing an expensive product/service and you need to produce an interesting document to attract attention, so that the people who read it (the purchasers) want to meet you, and give you the opportunity to sell. You do not need a full biography which someone has to dredge through in the faint hope of finding something vaguely interesting to read; it does not have to be complete in every detail. It does have to meet fairly stringent criteria of honesty and integrity – but mainly it must be something that is *exciting for the reader*. You need to create some anticipation or expectation of 'good news' to get the reader saying 'Here's someone I'd really like to meet and/or find out about.'

It must be a strong introduction to people who have not met you before, with the aim of intriguing them enough to want to interview or meet you. The CV won't get you a new job; it cannot – when selecting candidates for a new job, nearly everyone will want to meet them or assess them personally in some way. The CV is the first step along the way. When you get to the interview, you can fill in some of the detail.

What a good CV can and does do is help the interviewer decide whether or not to invite you in for an interview. Usually the CV will arrive before you – and it may be the only view of you that someone gets (if they are unimpressed by it). Often this is the case when applying for a new job. Your CV arrives, doesn't meet the reviewer's needs and you get a formal rejection letter – or nothing at all. Perhaps it has become 'junk mail' – irrelevant, uninteresting, as before. So your CV must be an **exciting personal introduction** to someone whom you are keen to meet.

Next, the CV will often serve as an **interview prompt sheet** for interviewers, who will almost certainly read it carefully before meeting you to assess your experience, and may make notes on it of questions they wish to ask. Interviewers may refer to it during your interview, for example saying 'You say in your CV that you ...' So, if it is going to be a prompt sheet, you must prompt the right questions – the answers to which sell you well. The interviewer may also make notes on the CV as the interview progresses – as you answer his prepared questions or questions on wholly different topics which have come up in discussion, i.e. using the CV as a notepad.

The CV also forms a **preparation document for you** for an

interview. You know in advance that the interviewer is very likely to refer to a copy of your CV, possibly having it on the desk at the time, and you can also use it beforehand to prepare what you want to say in the interview. There will be various work references in it – you can and must ensure that you have the necessary details (time, place, amount/volume etc) to hand, as well as what you did in the job to cause things to happen. I suggest that you prepare short (lasting 1½ to 3 minutes or so) 'skill stories' to expand on the key points in your CV to show how you actually did make a difference – and what the effect was. Then, when asked about them, you will have the basics of a ready-made response to hand.

The next role for the CV comes after you leave. **Interviewers will probably refer to your CV afterwards** to remind them of you, your experience, and your interview performance. They may well show it, complete with (possibly detailed and scruffy!) notes about you taken during the interview, to colleagues or to 'the boss', describing you as 'one of …', or perhaps even 'the best of the people I interviewed.' The CV needs to be a **quick and effective reminder of you** – and any third party also needs a good introduction to you (as referred to above).

You may be aware of other opportunities for bringing yourself to the attention of people who could be useful to you in finding a new role or roles, temporary assignment(s), interim job(s), or consultancy work. The CV will be a vital part of your marketing 'armoury' in addressing these opportunities.

So there are a number of purposes that the CV must meet but the **key thing to remember** is that *it is not an accurate and complete listing of your career but a marketing document designed principally to attract interest* and cause people to make contact with you, or at least be keen to meet you and respond to your calls.

2.3 – Style and content

Put very simply, whatever choices you make about how your CV looks and what you include in it, the completed document must be appropriate to meet the above purposes for your readers. The style and content must help the readers to find the information they need easily, quickly, and in a way that generates enthusiasm. There are various types and styles of CV and you may decide to have more than one CV to meet the different needs that you face. In thinking about preparing your CV, your purpose should not be to 'get it done quickly' but to decide on style, content and presentation to best **meet the needs of your target market** and ensure that you are seen.

Every aspect of presentation can help – or hinder – your marketing and after you have prepared your new CV, part of your campaign will be to test-market it with a few people to get their comments. The document into which you will have put so much work will be the 'best you can do' at that stage, but you still need market feedback to help you assess what the market actually wants (see 2.4 below).

You will need to select a style, or a combination of styles, that suits you and the job you do, which gives a clear presentation, and one which (very similarly to mainstream marketing literature) sets out clearly **what you can do for the reader** in a way that **appeals to that reader.**

You will need it to focus mainly on your 'work career', with the most recent job set out in some detail and the further back you go into your career, the more in 'soft focus' or briefer details you will provide. The CV will need to cover the jobs held, organisations and dates, and the positive differences you made, together with some personal background such as education and other interests.

There is no one type of CV which works perfectly for every occasion. In nearly all cases, your CV will be accompanied by a letter, which can be used to increase the focus on meeting the readers' expressed or latent needs.

2.4 – Change

As you work your way through the next few weeks using your new CV, people may offer you advice on it. Some of this will be useful, some prejudiced, some possibly incorrect. However, when receiving this advice, it's best not to defend your 'beautifully crafted CV' but to accept and acknowledge all comments. If you defend it then and there, it's likely to cause the other person to dry up and you may miss some real pearl of wisdom. Record all feedback and consider it later, in your own office or home, and then decide what you will do with it. As a result of this feedback, it may be worth amending the CV you are using, but you should not change it regularly week by week. Try initially to get the 'best CV you can' (which will include getting advice on it from all around you prior to coming up with the final version) and then stick with it. Then perhaps consider every 3-6 months whether or not to change it, to take account of other people's feedback.

Chapter 2 – Key points

- The main purpose of your CV is to market you effectively.

- Understand clearly the various purposes of your CV, and then think about how best you can meet them – all at the same time!

- Start thinking about the style of CV that you might use – and jot down a few ideas that appeal. If possible, collect some CVs from other people for reference.

- Remember this is a long term project. The first CV you come up with is unlikely to be the best.

[add in your own learning points here]

-
-
-

3

Your Customers and Their Needs

3.1 – Introduction

In this chapter, I want to focus on the primary people who are going to be reading your CV. If you can identify and then meet their needs, you will stand a much better chance of moving yourself up the recruitment ladder towards an interview, which relies on getting through the first 'sift' of CVs. No doubt there are many points you want to get across in your CV, but the key thing is to **meet the reader's needs** rather than to say what you want to say.

So who is going to use your CV, what will they use it for, and what are they looking for? Who are your key readers and what are their requirements?

3.2 – The professional recruiter

Recruitment organisations (which come in a variety of forms) sit between you and your potential employer. They provide a range of services for the recruiting employer – from sending mailshots of available people to managing nearly all of the recruitment process including interviews. There are many reasons why employers use a recruiter but here we just need to consider what the recruiter's special needs are because often you will be sending them your CV, not sending it to the employer. The recruiters have virtually full control over whether or not you 'get through' to the employer, so they are key!

Recruiters are in business to provide an efficient, reliable, and cost-effective service to **their clients (i.e. the recruiting employers, not you)**, on a profitable basis for themselves. They are not in business to satisfy your needs – they are **not even there to help you** towards meeting your needs. If they do help you, it's either incidental to achieving their client's needs, or part-fulfilling their own needs, or by pure chance. They receive hundreds of CVs per month from people seeking jobs – for example, these days they may receive 400 CVs for each manager-level job advertised – plus many more that are sent in daily on a speculative basis. They have little time to scan each individual CV – giving perhaps 30-60 seconds to each in their initial appraisal. They become experts in CV appraisal with similar overall requirements, but they are also likely to have their own personal preferences about what they want and don't want as well.

Generally, what recruiters want is a **clear presentation of the facts** they need to enable them to prepare a shortlist to send to the client of good prospects for the position being recruited.

☒ They are not interested in struggling through masses of detailed information and trying to evaluate who the writer of the CV is or whether there might be a good fit.

☒ Nor are they necessarily looking for the 'very best fit' person.

☑ They are looking to find someone who is a safe bet, someone who fits well, or even very well, where there are no real doubts, gaps or worrying bits of information.

☑ Provided they get a very good shortlist, the client will be pleased – even if the shortlist misses out the 'ideal person' because that person couldn't prepare a decent CV.

The recruiters will make the first decision based on your CV – does it tell enough about you and can they find that out with ease and pleasure? Can they put you forward with confidence?

As professional readers of CVs, recruiters (and their researchers) get very good at picking out the salient information – as well as finding any gaps. They will be comparing your CV with many others they receive for basic facts, layout, and information.

- Is it interesting?
- Easy to read?
- Good English?
- Does it 'talk their language'?
- Correct spelling and grammar?
- Too short/long?
- Well laid out?
- Does it have all the necessary information?
- Is it relevant?
- Is it annoying/irritating?

Recruiters are particularly critical of 'spin' (i.e. trying to talk up your achievements). The key information they need is – **what has the candidate done, for whom, when, and who can prove it?**

3.3 – The recruiting employer

If the employer has used a recruiter to conduct part or most of the recruitment campaign, the employing manager will at some stage see your CV – but only after it has (possibly) been 'doctored' by the recruiter. In any event, by then you will have been put on the short-list of 4 to 6 'likely choices' prepared by the recruiter (or maybe a long-list of 12 to 20 'possibles'). Your CV will have met the tests for the recruiter (see 3.2 above) but will still be reviewed in some detail subsequently by the employer.

For employers advertising directly themselves, your CV will be reviewed either by the recruiting manager or by the HR department (or both). Many of the criteria of choice that they will use are similar to those of the recruiter, but the recruiting manager is likely to have less experience of reviewing CVs than either the company's HR department or the recruiter. On the positive side, the recruiting managers are the ones actually making the hiring decisions and could be attracted to 'just the right candidate' (in their eyes). They do have their own 'agenda'.

Reviews by the recruiting managers do have one major advantage for you – theirs is not a short-term interest. Whereas (putting it very harshly) the recruiters or the company HR departments are interested principally in the short-term hiring decision, the recruiting managers have to run their departments over time, i.e. they have a long-term interest in getting the right person. They are also more able to pick a 'wild card' from the applying candidates or to reshape their requirements to fit around someone seen as a real 'potential asset for the department or business who does not quite match the original specification'.

So, can they pick out the necessary information about you from your CV – how you will make a radical and positive difference to their departments or businesses? Or is finding the information a struggle? Are your major skills, achievements and so on very clearly identified?

3.4 – Your network of contacts

Part of your campaign to find a new job should involve talking to people who know you, who have worked with you, or for you, or for whom you have worked, or possibly who are going to be referees for you. You may well be asking them for advice on your plans and activities and many of them will almost certainly ask to see your CV. Whilst it goes without saying that your CV must reflect the truth, your network will almost certainly know the truth – so don't be tempted to exaggerate or worse!

You can use your CV to **remind your network of your expertise and experience**. Asking for advice on your CV is a good conversation opener, because most people like to offer advice – and giving advice on a CV can be easy! It's not seen as 'personal criticism' and most people have some firm ideas on at least part of the CV – how it's written, presented/laid out and so on. It's also a good way to remind your referees and contacts just how good you are and of the things you have done. Many of your contacts will know about some parts of your career/life, but probably not all aspects. However, a review of your CV is an opportunity for you to set out your key skills and achievements to people who may later be asked about you, and then for you to discuss your employability with them in some detail. So, if you want them to be able to 'flow with good information' when they talk to others about you, get busy now with a bit of pump-priming by giving them a clear and positive presentation.

3.5 – You yourself

The preparation of your CV should give you the opportunity to consider the wide range of skills, talents, abilities and experience you have available to offer the market. If you do the preparation well, it should have the effect of boosting your self-esteem and confidence and when you have finished preparing your CV, you should be really proud that it markets you well to whoever reads it. It should give you a 'morale boost' to enable you to get out there and market yourself positively and effectively. That is one serious purpose of the CV – **to make you feel good about selling yourself**.

Use the CV as a 'checklist' prior to an interview – interviewers are likely to say 'You've said in your CV that you … Can you tell me about it?' So make sure that the things you want to talk about are mentioned in your CV and that you are prepared to talk about them at interview!

3.6 – General requirements

Most people reading your CV will have a **specific interest** to evaluate or check out, or a job specification to match with a candidate's details. In either case, they will want to feel reassured by your CV that you can meet their requirements. You will need to put yourself in their shoes to understand those requirements and then find a way to meet their needs.

Readers of your CV (who will also be reviewing many others at the same time) will want to follow up and meet with a small percentage of the people described – who will be potential candidates. They will be making the **'Yes'**, **'Maybe'**, or **'No'** decisions about whether or not to meet the person described each time that they read a CV. My view is that to aim to get to 'Yes' every time may be too big a challenge – you need to aim for a **'definite maybe'**!

Some of your readers will not be industry experts; so it is a good idea for you to keep the language general and not to use too many technical or specialist terms, which may not be understood. They need to be able to read through quickly, picking up key information easily – which they cannot do if they don't understand some key words. You 'never get a second chance to make a first impression' so make it count the first time.

When reviewing your CV, most readers will be looking for information about the organisations for which you have worked, in what capacity you were engaged, your responsibilities and what you have done to create a better, more efficient, profitable organisation. They will be looking for **signs of progression** – in responsibility, staff supervised, project size, and money. If in doubt, they are likely to take the 'safe bet', a good option, a 'reliable pair of hands', or some such. They are unlikely to choose a 'wild card' in order to explore whether this may give a better option – the safe option is likely to be preferred in most cases.

As a marketing document, **your CV needs to promote you well**. If you read other marketing materials, you will see that undue modesty is generally not a feature but, in quality materials, neither is hype. Honesty about where you have been and what you have done is required and in my view, there is a place for due pride in presenting a fair picture. As the saying goes – if you can't say something good about yourself, who can!

There is something about work or the job-search process that makes us all want to be either unduly modest, or (worse) exceptionally up-front and outspoken about our failings. If you imagine meeting your life partner for the first time – are you really going to say immediately that you snore noisily and have several speeding offences? You will probably wait until you have made a good impression before bringing out the dirty washing! Your CV is your personal advertisement and needs to impress without being untruthful – don't be too modest and certainly don't volunteer your dirty washing at this stage!

Most people in preparing their own CV will:

- miss out some key skills and achievements

- not take realistic/full credit for what they have done

- include too much detail, making the key information hard to find

- insist on pointing out weaknesses or attributes/experience which are desired (but not required) by the advertiser which they, the candidates, do not have.

Chapter 3 – Key points

- To be effective, your CV must stand out from the mass of CVs received.

Make it special.

- Your CV should be focused on meeting the reader's needs, not just on what you want to say. If you wrote an application letter saying, 'I love the sound of the job, it will be good for my career, the salary is excellent and the fringe benefits superb,' you'd be unlikely to get the job – because the letter is focused solely on what you want. Instead, you have to tell the readers what they want to hear – how your skills meet their needs, why your experience is very close to their requirements, the huge positive difference you can make from day one, and the benefits you bring for them.

- At the end of any review of your CV, the recruiter or employer is going to make a 'Yes', 'Maybe' or 'No' decision. Modesty is fine in moderation but you cannot take the view that your career 'speaks for itself'. You must talk about yourself in a way that persuades an employer that you are worth looking at!

- Remember that the reader is saying to himself, 'What's in it for me?'

4

Marketing Yourself

4.1 – Introduction

As your prime marketing document, your CV is like any other
marketing document sent out on behalf of a product or service. The
key purpose is to excite interest, to persuade someone to pick up the
phone, or respond to a phone call, and to want to set up a meeting. It
is very hard to sell to someone who is not already interested in the
product/service you want to sell; you must interest them first and
create the opportunity to sell. Let's look at how you can generate
greater interest.

4.2 – Marketing versus selling

There is much confusion in business about the difference between
marketing and selling. The definition I use is that marketing is the
process by which you attract a potential customer's interest to your
product or service and selling is what you do to encourage that
customer to commit to the purchase, once you have attracted his
attention.

So, in CV or job-seeking terms, the marketing is what happens
before you meet someone to discuss any particular job. **You need to
position yourself as the 'preferred supplier'** (or, at least, as one of
the preferred suppliers) with a potential customer. How do you make
your 'product' attractive and interesting to your customer? Look at

other marketing material and see how it provides (or perhaps does not provide?) a clear description of what the product does for the user, how it helps, how easy it is to use, how well it meets the needs, and how many people recommend it.

Selling is what you do when you are in front of 'buyers' or on the phone to them once they have decided that they are interested in talking to you or in meeting you. Enhancing your skills in the sales process (i.e. moving through a series of interviews towards a job offer) is a whole new subject – you may want to consider improving your telephone and interview skills. It is, however, outside the scope of this book.

4.3 – Reader focus

Your CV is a relatively short presentation of your work, your achievements, your life history and so on, but in practical terms, to be effective as a marketing tool for you, it must have a strong reader focus. It's about **demonstrating benefits to the reader** – i.e. what the reader of your CV wants to see.

4.4 – Why you need marketing

Just like any other product in a crowded marketplace, you are facing serious competition. If you don't market yourself well, your readers (or 'potential buyers') will not be sufficiently impressed by your CV to want to follow up with a meeting or phone call; they won't put you 'on the list'. They may be more interested in some of the other CVs they have received which are more focused on their needs.

Strong marketing performance is also a requirement because you are facing a major constraint. Most people receiving your CV will allocate a very short time to the first appraisal of it. You need to make a big impression quickly, which you do by producing a clear and focused CV which meets the reader's needs.

Another aspect of marketing is that there may be people 'out there' who could need your services, but of whom you are unaware (and who may therefore be totally unaware of you). Your CV can be passed to them by someone else, as being of potential interest, the transfer being made without your knowledge. You therefore need to be sure that the CV stands alone (i.e. without you) to make a generally convincing impression of you as being someone who is interesting, who makes a difference, and who should be met, talked to or whatever. You want other people to be able to open doors for you – because they have read your CV, found it easy to read, understand, and remember, and are thoroughly impressed by you.

4.5 – Skills

One of the main things you bring to a new employer is your package of transferable skills. Wherever you come from in terms of career experience, whether newly out of school or college, or after 20 years in a career, you will have developed a range of skills. The particular mix of skills is yours, but what you now need to do is understand what your skills are and be able to present them in various ways as part of the 'service pack' you are offering. Before we spend time on preparing a list of your transferable skills and experience, start thinking now about what you have done or do regularly and how it might be applied somewhere else.

What we'll cover later is establishing what these skills are, the evidence for this, how to refine the description, how to define the skills and then to illustrate them in action in a way that becomes interesting to the reader or interviewer.

4.6 – Experience

The second major area of benefit that you will be offering to your 'purchasers' is the experience you have gained in using your package of skills in your work (and possibly other experience areas). Think of what you have achieved in these areas in projects, leading teams, developing new ideas/plans and so on. What were the sizes, numbers, and/or market positions? Were you the 'first/largest/fastest in industry'? What did you do to 'be the hero'?

It may be appropriate to think about how your experience shows growth (in numbers of ... etc) in the job, responsibilities and so on, and how you are meeting your ambitions.

Then consider what you have done outside the immediate work environment. Sometimes, pastimes or voluntary work can demonstrate further application of skills outside work – or it may show new skills which you do not use currently in your employment.

4.7 – Market research

Market research is a vital part of marketing – finding out what your target customers want and do not want. In the retail marketplace, millions are spent every year to help market products and services more effectively. If you were working for an organisation that was bringing out a new product, the firm would have conducted a fair amount of market research to see that what they were selling met the market requirements – and then would ensure that the marketing materials clearly pointed out the key information on how these market needs could be met.

It's not so easy to conduct market research into what the needs are of the people who might employ you. However, you can improve your knowledge of the market requirements of you and your CV. For example, I'm sure you will be looking at advertisements. Don't confine yourself solely to those of direct interest to you for employment. In reviewing other advertisements, you may come across useful information about jobs or organisations, about recruiter requirements and such like, to help you with assembling your CV. Look particularly at the language used, any special phrases, or technical issues. Think about researching the industry sector you wish to join. Consider what makes a good banker, lawyer, finance director, or manager.

You are seeking to build up your knowledge of the marketplace.

Talk to people you know, especially those who see other people's CVs more than once. Find out what makes them interested in people who write to them and conversely, what makes their blood boil! See what they think of your draft CV and make a note of their comments.

And, as a bit of 'lateral thinking', take a closer look at your 'junk mail'. This may not seem directly relevant, but direct mail marketing is one of the best researched industries around. For that letter to arrive in your letter-box, you will have been targeted for a reason – the sender has established by research that you are strongly likely to be interested. This view will be founded on database analysis and matching your recorded interests with the product or service offered. In looking at the 'junk mail' letter, consider why you want to read it – and/or why you do not. What makes it attractive to you? What words or presentations work? Are there any tips you can carry across to your CV?

Chapter 4 – Key points

- A CV is not just a presentation of facts – it's about attracting someone's interest to you with factual information to give you the chance to do something, especially to create an opportunity to sell yourself.

- Marketing is about meeting the readers' needs, not your own. What are they looking for?

- You are working in an extremely competitive market. Nothing but the best will do.

- It's no use being over-modest. You must market yourself well and effectively, taking due credit for your skills, experience and achievements.

-

-

-

5

Data Collection and Analysis

5.1 – Introduction

Okay, enough of the theory – let's get started! This chapter is about how you can collect data about you, your skills and experience, and about your work. It's about how to assemble raw data on you, the organisations you have worked for (full time, part time or in a voluntary capacity), and your achievements in those roles. Your data collection and analysis need to cover a wide range of work experience and to be instrumental in building a picture of you that attracts positive attention.

You may say 'Why do I need to collect data – I know all the important information?' The reason, essentially, is that you (as with most of us) probably know all the information that you currently think is important to you. What you need to do now is collect data in order to be able to sort out key information that is **important to the reader of your CV.** Rest assured, most people (before training and preparation) are bad at selling themselves; even professional sales people who are excellent at selling products/services in their jobs can be very bad at selling themselves. I'm suggesting that you approach the task as methodically as if you were selling a new company's new product – one which you had never seen before. Amass the data, analyse it, decide what is important, what will interest potential customers, and then prepare the literature.

5.2 – Assembling the raw data

Time spent collecting data is rarely wasted. I suggest that you set aside a couple of days to research your career – both from your own sources and externally. Approach the data collection in two ways. Firstly, summarise, on a separate sheet of paper, each job that you have had in your career so far, under (at least) the following headings:

1   Job title.

2   Your boss' job title and the name of the team.

3   Details of the employer (name/location/business etc).

4   Dates of employment (month/year, start/finish).

5   The responsibilities of your job, giving as much quantification as possible.

6   Your most significant contributions and achievements in that job.

7   In 5 and 6 above, include numbers of people supervised, size of department (or whatever you ran), volumes produced or sold, other measures of your performance.

8   Remuneration (initial/final, bonus, other benefits).

9   Reasons for accepting the job.

10 Reasons for leaving.

11 Simple organisation chart showing your position, to whom you reported and your direct reports.

Try to include as much descriptive information as possible about your roles, so that it will be available for you to analyse and consider for the CV – and also because interviewers often ask for this type of information. You may need to dig out old files, talk to former colleagues etc. to fill in the blanks. If the information is (potentially) sensitive or confidential, I'm not suggesting that you will give it to anyone else in that form – the data collection is for your own needs. However, it is still important to record it, as it will help you now to consider how to talk about the information later if asked.

Secondly, think about the things you have done both inside and outside of work that you have enjoyed, done well, and of which you were/are proud; I call these **'achievements'**. These do not have to be major, world-shaking events, just things that you did (on your own or with others) about which you can say 'I did that'. I often say to my clients 'Think of things that might be said at a presentation about you, at your retirement, or things that you might say to your children' (or even 'things that might appear in your obituary'!). Try to get as much descriptive information down about them – what, where, when, how much, how big and so on. Ask 'What difference did I make?'

Think of those things you have done and how all or part of them might be relevant to any new job. For instance, if you have helped raise money for a charity in your spare time, did you organise it? If you won a sailing race – were you the captain and how did you manage the crew? Had you just learned a new skill? How have you contributed to these successes? (If you really have difficulties finding many such achievements, then start tomorrow looking for how you can involve yourself in activities that could be of use.) Most of us have achievements, it's just that very few of us have learned how to speak about our achievements and take due credit for them.

It's easy to say, 'Well, I can remember that if someone asks,' but that doesn't help you in writing about yourself now and you may be able to improve your presentation later by some preparation now. Most people need a couple of days to do this properly – writing down, and then coming back to it a few times to provide a reasonably complete picture. Sometimes, completing the 'achievements' part of the above exercise adds things the first parts (items 1 to 11 in the above list), which can then prompt further additions to the achievements. In the first draft, don't worry too much about completeness and accuracy – that can be tidied up later – just get as much down as possible.

5.3 – Checking the data

There may be some missing information that you need to complete the above which will not be immediately available to you and other information where you may not be sure of your facts. Research as much as you can from your memory and from your old files, from talking to friends or former colleagues and perhaps researching their files, and from public sources such as the internet or public libraries. There are bound to be some items where you really cannot get at the information, and it may be appropriate to prepare estimates or approximations. In my view it is better (if you cannot remember that it was, say, 19.4 million) to say 'It was about 20 million' rather than to say 'I really cannot remember'. It is the order of magnitude that is relevant rather than the exact number or date or whatever.

You will want to ensure that you have a complete record of what you have done, where and when, so don't be tempted to leave out short periods of which you are less than proud. We'll talk later about how to deal with such information later. This really is a bit like preparing a life history!

5.4 – Refining and analysing the data

One of the more important parts of the data preparation comes at the second stage in trying to assemble the right information in the right way to impress and interest. Assembling and now reviewing this package of information enables you to spot trends or themes running through your past record. Try underlining key verbs/words, or writing notes in the margins on **what you actually did to make things happen**. See if certain phrases or verbs keep cropping up – showing the sort of things you do regularly. Check the listing of action words in Section 6.4 to see which can apply to you.

After each paragraph or achievement, try to summarise your input in the form of 'What was the problem, what were the implications, what did I do, and what was the result?'

One of the key things you will want to present to potential new employers is a menu of transferable key skills. As you review your record, see if certain skills reappear in successive jobs or assignments.

Chapter 5 – Key points

- Collect as much information as you reasonably can about your career and experience so far. If you cannot measure it exactly, make a reasonable estimate.

- Make sure that the information you have collected about you is as correct as possible and builds the right picture.

- Spend much more time on the successes than on the failures or omissions – you are unlikely to be offered a job on the basis of what you cannot do well!

-

-

-

6

The Basic Rules

6.1 – Introduction

Although there are a number of different styles for a CV, there are some basic rules governing presentation and content that apply to any CV destined for 'publication'. Some of these may seem obvious, but I have written them here with the benefit of long experience – you would be surprised at some of the CVs I have seen – e.g. ones without either the name or address of the 'owner'!

6.2 – The basic rules

Here are some basic rules about writing your CV – in no particular order of importance:

Theme
The overall CV needs to have a theme. You are trying to create an impression with this document – so it needs to look like you, feel like you, be like you, with the overall theme being you in the new job. So, if you are an accountant aiming to be a finance director, that's what it needs to sound like – you in the role of finance director. If you are a sales person, it needs to sound like a sales CV. If you state that you are accurate and financially orientated, energetic and deliver results, then the whole CV needs to be a reflection of this. Woe betide you if you say 'I communicate well' or 'I am good at presentations' if your CV does not communicate or present well!

Appearance/presentation

The CV needs to be attractive to pick up. Spend a few minutes now writing down what causes you to pick up a piece of mail from the desk/floor with enthusiasm to read it.

It should be presented on white paper, printed on one side only, neatly typed/word-processed, with all punctuation, spelling, spacing, and English grammar correct. Do not rely on the spell- and grammar-checkers included with your PC – they are not context-sensitive and you could find your CV mistakenly contains a similar word, correctly spelled, meaning something completely different e.g. 'As a result, my team was sued' (instead of 'my team was used').

Choose a commonly-used typeface or font such as Times Roman (as the paragraphs in this book) or Arial (as the headings) rather than for example, **Benquiat Bk BT** – however startling the latter may appear. Your readers are (relatively) conservative and the typeface should meet their needs. The most common view is that a sans-serif font (e.g. like Arial) is not as easy to read as one with serifs (e.g. Times Roman) so bear this in mind too. You can mix fonts within a document e.g. to clarify information. The font size must be readable (probably minimum 11 point – like this book) and the use of printing features such as bold, underline, upper-case, margins, tabs, boxes, bullets and italic should help the reader to get to relevant and related information, focus on the important, and improve understanding.

Allow plenty of white space around the printed material to allow for clear appearance and for note-taking. Do not use binders, laminations, covers, title page or separation sheets – which all add weight and clutter without adding to the positive impression for your readers.

The overall layout should 'group' relevant information together to help the reader – for example, achievements within all your jobs could be set out with the same style bullet points. All organisations for which you have worked should be listed in the same typeface, point size, and 'bold'ing. All information about one job should be grouped together, then leaving a slightly larger space before the next heading/job. Use separate 'sections' for career details, education, and personal information.

Important information should attract more attention than the less important – e.g. if you use the heading 'Career' it is probably less important than your name and the names of the organisations for which you have worked – so its presentation should be less important (smaller point size, not bold, italic or whatever).

The impression given should be top quality – after all, that is what you are selling!

Length

The current 'accepted standard' for the length of a CV is **two to three pages**. The definition 'two pages' also covers a one page CV with a three page appendix – because if the first page is a complete history and excites interest, the reader will go on to read all four pages. The reader's interest is the key driver. (I still recall a 'wonderful' CV I received many years ago – 52 pages long, with covers, drawings, summary patent applications, all neatly laid in the form of a report. However, it didn't meet my needs as a reader but I'm afraid it did meet my criteria of being very easy to 'ditch'. A great shame for the writer, who had put in so much hard but misguided work!)

Okay, so you've read the above advice and yet you still want a 'proper CV with all the details'. I can't stop you doing so, but in my experience, professional readers of CVs just do not have time to read a six-page document and then winnow out the salient or key facts that they need. True, you may get one or two readers who love the length and detail (I have had one client produce eight closely typed pages in 9-point font, printed double-sided, and one recruiter said 'Great!') But, the odds will work against you finding a reader who is so different from the norm. It's better to start with a short punchy document and have the detail available should someone want it.

Out of 400 CVs for each job advertised, maybe 30 will rate more than a swift glance before rejection and after a second slightly longer look, perhaps twelve will be considered in depth and maybe eight interviewed. The weight alone of six pages makes it easy to reject – so make it easy to pick you by fitting in with the accepted requirements.

If you are finding it almost impossible to condense your CV into 'about two pages', my remaining suggestion is to get a friend, mentor, coach, or 'someone else' you trust, to go through the CV removing anything they feel is not critically important. Involving another person can bring objectivity as you try to justify why you want to include certain information. If you really are stuck, then the way forward may be to have a summary page (profile, company/organisations, jobs list, education, personal) with the detailed presentation coming in for pages 2 to 4/5.

Content

The content of your CV should be **appropriate to you** and your experience (see 'theme' above). Don't be tempted to be 'clever' – for example, a sales person including detailed accounting issues (unless it is relevant and you really can support this in an interview).

Relevance is important – if you are a PA/secretary, it may be useful to put your experience of using various word-processing packages; if you are a senior manager, 'computer literate' is probably sufficient; the alternative of giving much more detail of your experience in using Word and Excel may give the wrong impression.

Quantify (i.e. use numbers to show size) and **qualify** (the biggest, best, first, largest in Europe etc) as much as you can to create the right picture.

In describing the **impact** you have on an organisation, if you use 'action words' (see section 6.4) such as 'doing', 'building', delivering', 'ensuring', it can be more interesting that the past tense 'did', 'built', 'delivered', 'ensured' as well as giving a sense of continuing or ongoing achievement. At other times, the past tense can be right, e.g. solidly confirming an achievement.

'English'

For the content, I always favour using 'short-form' English rather than totally 'proper' sentence construction. By this I mean that saying *'Achieved a 20% increase in sales and doubled profit'* is quicker and more interesting to read than, *'I built up the sales over the year to almost 20% higher than in the previous year and because I controlled expenditure, it resulted in profits nearly doubling in the same period'*.

The first is easier to read and appreciate or retain, conveys more, and takes up much less space!

If there's one thing that's guaranteed to upset readers of CVs, it's incorrect spelling and grammar. It comes out in nearly every conversation with professional recruiters on 'CVs that irritate'!

Style

As well as writing short sharp phrases in your CV, you should ensure that the overall style is easy to read and approachable. You are out to make life easy for your readers, to make them want to pick your CV in preference to others, to read it, and to retain it etc. It should be positive, upbeat, specific, to the point, honest, and with an action focus.

Delivery

A few years ago, there was little option but the normal postal system. Now, you have the option of mail, email, fax, or personal/courier delivery. I still feel that you should aim to produce an attractive hard copy of your CV – but some recruiters will ask you to send your CV by email. In the latter case, I would suggest sending it as an attachment to your email rather than in the text of the email – because otherwise you are likely to lose all the formatting in your CV presentation. You may also want to follow up with hard copy by post (certainly I would suggest this if you fax the CV to the reader).

There is also the question of CVs being scanned into computers – with the recommendation that you leave out bold text, italics, underlining, boxes etc. Again, I would still recommend that you prepare your CV on the basis that the hard copy is the important use (but if you know it's going to be scanned, re-present the information as suggested/requested).

Order of presentation

I know it's obvious, but the front page of your CV sits on top and is the first thing the reader sees. It therefore needs to contain the most important information about you. I believe that in addition, the key 'sales area' is the top half of that top sheet. (If you look at a piece of

A4, it's very hard to take in the full sheet at one glance). So in writing up your career in your CV, work from the most recent role/job backwards and ensure especially that the first half page is thoroughly impressive! Spend more time/space on the most recent job and use progressively less space to record details of each job as you go further back – and consider consolidating your early years (more than 10-12 years ago) into one paragraph to give you more space to present the detail of the later years. (See also 'appearance/presentation' regarding the grouping of key information).

Truth

What you put in your CV must be truthful, but there are often different ways of saying the same thing. For example, to say, *'I have very limited experience in using Excel'* could be expressed as *'Commenced training course to develop my Excel skills'*, but the latter is more interesting! Information included must however be true. Don't put in negative information (lack of this, failure at that) – everyone has them, but the CV is not the place to put them. By all means think about how you can present this information orally if and when you need to (e.g. what you learned as a result of the failure). See 6.3 below.

Meeting the 30-90 second rule

The reviewer will (initially at least) have a very limited time to pick up the key information about you from the CV. If someone is trying to review 400 CVs, and is taking only 60 seconds to read each, that makes up a full day's work! So they are unlikely in the first instance to spend longer than (say) 30-90 seconds reading your CV for the first time. You have to create a good impression on that individual within 60 seconds – so does your CV make the grade? Is it crisp and clear?

Pride

It's critical that you 'own' your CV and take pride in what it says about you, and how it describes you. Many cultures teach that talking about ourselves is 'not nice' and as a result of this background we tend to underplay our strengths, skills, achievements and contributions. Modesty has its place, but not in a marketing document! I like the idea of what one client said to me – 'You need a good honest conceit' when writing the CV. That's not to say it can be full of hype – it's just that it must clearly make the points about you that you want to make that will cause the reader to want to meet you to hear more. Underplaying it does not work.

Responsibilities and achievements

It's a good idea to show both responsibilities and achievements in your CV – but to spend more time/space on the latter, because the former would probably be the same for your predecessor and successor – the achievements tell a lot about you. You should use the layout to help the reader and so I suggest that you use one layout for all responsibilities and a different layout for all your achievements. For example, you might consider using a normal paragraph layout for your key responsibilities and then have a longer section of bullet points for the key achievements. In each case, you would reduce the amount of detail when describing earlier jobs.

Abbreviation

However good you are, or however short your career, you are going to have limited space for what you want to say, so take most opportunities to abbreviate words or information. Obviously, don't put in large numbers in full (1,200,000 is better written as 1.2m) and similarly with other common abbreviations, but if you need to refer a number of times to a long phrase or name, say, Management Books 2000 Limited, put ('MB2000') after the first use of the name or phrase and then use MB2000 thereafter.

6.3 – The missing bits

In saying that you have to be honest in your CV, I recognise that this can also go too far! It's very tempting to draw attention to what you haven't got in the interests of being comprehensive. Don't do it! When you're thinking of buying a new car and you look at a brochure for a luxury coupé, you don't see straight away 'this car may be too small for you and your family' because the vendor is thinking, 'Well it might not be, there might be another option'. He wants to meet you to discuss the possibilities (in the best case perhaps to sell you a coupé and an estate!). Similarly, if you are invited to the first interview, you may be able to convince your interviewer that the overall 'package' you have available is better for the business than those of other applicants (even though you are currently missing one piece of the stated requirements).

One of the key things you must omit however is 'puff'! You will need to be outgoing about your skills and ability – and you must be prepared to state what you can do, what you are good at. There is no need to inflate what you have done – that only inspires disbelief. In due course, when you get to an interview, you will need to be able to back up your claims with relevant examples – and perhaps you will want to include a couple of examples in the CV itself. Do not include false claims!

6.4 – Action words

Here is a list of 'action words' that you may find useful in preparing your CV; use them either in the CV itself or to remind you of things you actually did. Work through the list to see what comes back into your mind about your career achievements.

Achieving	Administering	Analysing
Applying	Appraising	Assisting
Beating	Building	Chairing
Challenging	Closing down	Communicating
Complying	Computerising	Conducting
Conserving	Constructing	Contributing
Controlling	Converting	Convincing
Co-ordinating	Counselling	Creating
Cultivating	Cutting	Delivering
Designing	Developing	Devising

Directing	Drawing up	Driving
Ensuring	Establishing	Evaluating
Exceeding	Extending	Forecasting
Forming	Growing	Heading
Helping	Highlighting	Identifying
Implementing	Improving	Incorporating
Increasing	Influencing	Initiating
Installing	Integrating	Introducing
Investing	Launching	Leading
Licensing	Maintaining	Making (things happen)
Managing	Marketing	Meeting
Mentoring	Merging	Minimising
Motivating	Negotiating	Organising
Overcoming	Persuading	Planning
Preparing	Presenting	Prioritising
Problem-solving	Producing	Providing
Proving	Recommending	Reconciling
Recruiting	Reducing	Reorganising
Repairing	Repositioning	Representing
Researching	Revealing	Reviewing
Running	Selling	Servicing
Setting (up)	Sharing	Simplifying
Sourcing	Speaking	Standardising
Stimulating	Streamlining	Strengthening
Structuring	Taking over	Thriving
Training	Transforming	Underpinning
Understanding	Unifying	Using
Working	Writing	

6.5 – Stages of life

As you progress through your career, the CV you produce must change, e.g. your first CV as you leave school, college or university, is unlikely to contain much by way of jobs/positions held, work experience and sole responsibilities. The CV you produce at this time is going to be based on your education and perhaps some outside-of-work activities; this is unlikely to be appropriate for marketing you ten years later. Similarly, when you are approaching retirement, perhaps looking for voluntary work, your CV may require some fine-tuning to your new situation.

6.6 – How to start

You may be wondering 'Okay, how do I start – I thought I knew how to write a CV, but this is all new and I've got to get it into two pages!' I suggest you use the following order – after doing all the data collection and analysis set out in Chapter 5:

- Start by thinking about the content – what do you want to say to meet the reader's needs?

- Then look at the style of presentation that suits you.

- Finally pay attention to the length.

The basis for this is that it's in order of difficulty – getting the right content is hard; cutting it out later is much easier!

6.7 – Key points

Follow the basic rules.

- **Go for content, then style, then length.**
- **Keep it as simple as possible, impress with brevity.**
-
-
-

7

Getting People to Look at Your CV

7.1 Introduction

There are probably no general 'rules' to which recruiters and managers adhere when appraising CVs, so what I'm going to offer you are a personal set to help you assess how to prepare an effective CV to market you and your services.

I believe that the process by which you can help someone to pick up your CV (as opposed to selecting one of the many others received) and then appraise it so that you reach your goal of getting to the next stage of the meeting process, runs in four sequential steps:

1. The 'artistic' appearance
   - Do I want to pick this CV up?

2. Inviting the reader in
   - Shall I now spend time reading it in detail?

3. Fitting the person
   - Am I enjoying this read – and is it what I expect from someone at this level, this job, etc?

4. Walking away, is he a good fit?
   - Do I have a clear impression of this person? Does he seem right?

Let's look at each of these stages in turn.

7.2 – The artistic appearance

When we look at a piece of art, we are likely to appreciate it first in its totality to decide (probably fairly quickly) whether we like it or not; then we may decide to look at it more closely. Similarly, someone looking at your CV for the first time is likely to see it as an overall package, not immediately starting to read the words contained in it. The first judgement by your readers will be passed on the visual impression – the CV will be sitting on their desk, or will have come out of the envelope they have opened, and they will be deciding whether to pick it up and look further at it. You've been through the same process yourself – you look at the letter that's just fallen through your letterbox – a mass mailing – will you open it or what – and if you do, will you read it?

You need to consider the immediate impact of your CV's appearance on the recipient. Is the layout clear and presentable? Is it attractive or burdened with text? How long is it – does it create the impression 'This will be a good read' or 'Oh my – do I have to?' Does it ask the recipients to pick it up – or does it put them off? Does it seem to have the right sort of information? Is it distinctive (without being 'odd') or is it 'Just another boring CV'? Is it easy to read/skim, with a bit of originality?

A good test of this artistic appearance (if you have the materials to do it) is to assemble a number of CVs and lay them out on the floor. Then, when you walk into the room, which one catches your eye? Why? It is yours? Which is the easiest to pick up?

7.3 – Inviting the reader in

Let's now assume that the appearance has caught the recipient's eye – the next step is to invite the reader in to read the document in some detail. This requires a combination of things including the contents, the writing style, presentation of information, clarity of language, and clear 'signposting'. By signposting, I mean making it easy for the reader to reach the required information by using the same presentation for similar information, e.g. the same typeface and font size for all job titles, and grouping together all relevant information about the same topic, job or organisation. Is the CV clear and pertinent? Is the quality right (language, information, relevance) and is it well put together?

Readers have different needs, and all will want to assemble information in their own particular order. Your job at this stage is to present the information in a clear and logical manner – so that whatever the reader requires is easy to find. This is possibly a critical point – will the reader get 'sucked in' to read the information you have provided? Have you made it easy? If you get past this hurdle well, then the detailed review referred to in Section 7.4 will be that much easier to achieve.

At this stage, questions you would possibly want to ask the reader of your CV about it – if you were reviewing it together – would include:

- Is the information put together in a concise, clear, way?

- Is it easy to understand and is the information presented in such a way as to make it easy to get at what you want?

- Are the details sufficient or is there too much, is it clearly laid out – or confusing?

- Is it well articulated or are there some tired old clichés?

- Are there any major selling points?

- Does it help you in your job of reviewing CVs?

7.4 – Fitting the person

Having come through the initial appraisals, now the readers get into the real reading and analysis of your CV saying, 'Is this the sort of CV I would expect from someone with that background?'

The questions they might be asking themselves as they review the details are:

- Is it relevant and does it present a concise and clear picture of the candidate?
- Does it seem to be exaggerated?
- Are the achievements substantiated?
- Does it all hang together in a coherent way?
- Is it consistent across jobs and organisations?
- Is there sensible evidence of career progression, with sufficient measure of quantity and quality?
- Can I find the necessary skills and competences?
- Does it adequately spell out the achievements and do I believe them?
- Do any of the claims seem empty or over-stated?
- Are there any gaps or anomalies?

This is the 'meat and drink' of the CV review. No more or less important than the other three stages, but this is the one that most of us recognise fully. It's where the reviewer picks up most of the relevant information about you. Is it the right information? Does it match you and your career? Is your CV full of good solid demonstrable information and skills?

7.5 – Walking away – a good fit?

After concluding the initial 30-90 second critical appraisal, the reader will put the CV back on the desk and ask the critical questions:

- Do I have a clear picture of who this person is?

- What can the candidate do for me (or my client)?
- Does he fit the brief?
- How quickly will he be 'up to speed' in the new role?
- What's the feeling in my gut?
- Does he have any extra qualities?
- Do I want to meet him?

Have a look at the sample CVs in Appendix I and see how they meet the above criteria. Perhaps some do not – for you?

Chapter 7 – Key points

- Remember the top page of your CV creates the first impression and the top half of that page is the main 'sales area'.

- Think of the four appraisal steps – how does your CV stack up?

- Will your CV pass the 30-90 second test?

-

-

-

8

The Key Choices

8.1 – Introduction

Your CV will be read by a wide variety of people, mainly managers and recruiters, and you must bear their needs in mind – because you want to enthuse the managers who are recruiting for themselves and the recruiters who are the door or barrier between you and their client recruiting organisations. This chapter focuses on the choices that you will have to make as you prepare your CV – some being more significant than others, with some 'directed thinking' towards my own ideas where there are no clear answers!

8.2 – Should I have a 'profile'?

The section of a CV about which most people have a view, and which raises the temperature of arguments, is right at the top. This is where you will sometimes see a 'profile' or brief description of the person who is described in more detail in the rest of the CV. Some readers will find this type of statement absolutely objectionable, self-congratulatory, full of 'puff', and completely unnecessary; others will like it, saying it forms essential reading, gives them a very quick picture of the individual whose CV is set out below. The research I have seen has shown that in general, professional recruiters are more likely to prefer a CV without a profile, whereas the business or commercial managers definitely seem to prefer to read a profile.

Essentially, recruiters are acting as intermediaries and want to form their own impressions of you, before deciding whether or not to pass you on to their clients. They do this by reviewing the companies or organisations for which you have worked, the posts you have held, and what you have done on a regular basis to 'make a difference'. Recruiters will gain a quick impression from the CV appraisal, which (if they like it) is then developed further during one or more interviews. After this, they will want to prepare a profile themselves, in their own format, to send to their client – a profile which they will see as being prepared objectively by a third person (themselves).

Business managers on the other hand, want to gain a quick impression of who you are before they get into the details of the CV, asking themselves 'Is it worth going further with this – does it look as if they might be any good?' In market surveys I have seen, such managers have said in feedback that the profile is a vital piece of introductory information – providing it is written without self-aggrandisement and where what is said can be supported later in an interview.

So, should you have a profile or not? The choice is yours, but if in doubt, I'd suggest you include one, making sure that it is short, factual, and positive.

8.3 – How many CVs?

There are two widely-held and totally incompatible views on how many CVs you should have. One view, held by a number of 'industry experts', is that you should spend a lot of time preparing one CV that presents you as well as you possibly can – it's succinct, it's positive, it sells your skills well, and persuades people as much as possible that you are worth at least a second look. In any job application, you then send a letter to accompany this impressive general purpose CV and use the letter to 'tailor' the information in your CV to the job for which you are seeking to be interviewed.

The other view, equally valid and held by other 'experts', is that you should have a lengthy CV at home covering all your experience and achievements. You then extract from this document the key details relevant to each job for which you apply and prepare a specialised CV focused on the actual needs of the job. It still requires an introductory letter, which again can accentuate your key advantages/experience, and this approach has the advantage of putting a very strong case. It does however have three disadvantages (i) that you need to remember which CV you sent to whom – and may find the same person requiring/receiving different CVs, e.g. for different recruitment assignments; (ii) it requires a lot more work to tailor the CV as well as the letter to each job application; and (iii) it doesn't serve as a general purpose CV to send out if you don't know precisely what the recipient's interest is.

Both approaches have their merits, but if you really cannot decide, my biased opinion is to go for a single, general purpose CV and then, for each job specifically applied for, prepare an excellent covering letter which sets out exactly and briefly how you meet the advertised job requirements. It can still make a very strong sales 'package'.

A 'half-way house' approach that I have seen is where the main body of the CV covering the key skills and career experience has been left the same, but different profiles are used to bring out specific points in relation to different jobs or to meet individual requirements of the advertisement. It can also be used, for example, to introduce a role objective for a specific application.

This book is focused on 'writing a CV' – which is not meant to imply that you should only have one CV even though that is my 'fallback' option. Use the techniques described here for either a general CV or for the various CVs needed to match each job. In both cases you will need to analyse very carefully the job advertisement or job description to match up your sales package (letter + general CV) or (letter + specific CV) to the advertised job requirements.

My suggested approach for such **systematic analysis** is firstly, go through the advertisement/job specification carefully, e.g. identify by underlining in red the things that are said to be 'must haves' and then highlighting in green those that are 'desirable'. Once complete, make sure that (a) you can match up with at least 85% of the key 'must have' requirements and (b) that the letter and CV that you submit addresses all of the key 'must haves' and a few of the 'desirables' as well. With either type of CV, analyse the advertisement and research (including using the internet) to find out as much as you can about the organisation and the job, and then tailor the letter (and CV if you decide to have a job-specific one) to be as close a fit as you honestly can.

8.4 – Type of CV?

You will need to decide at a fairly early stage how you want to present the information about your career. There are a number of general layouts for CVs depending on which aspects of your career you wish to pull into focus. Within each overall style, other subsidiary styles are possible (e.g. within one job description, you could include your achievements as a list, or as bullet points, or as a paragraph). Any of the following styles could, if you wished, start with a profile.

8.4.1 – Jobs focus

The most common way of presenting the information is to focus on the jobs you have held giving details of your responsibilities and achievements. Start with the most recent job, giving it perhaps half a page and work backwards through your career giving less details the further back you go. This might start off looking like this:

BHP Ltd　　　　**Credit Controller**　　　　　**2002 - date**

Responsibilities: managing team of 12 qualified/part-qualified, to ...
　　　[descriptive paragraph]

Achievements:

- Reducing outstanding debtors from x to y weeks (worth £XXX)
- Performance managing my team
- Improving customer relationships

CVA Ltd　　　　**Credit Control Clerk**　　　1998 - 2002

Responsibilities:

Achievements:

-

Try to limit the responsibilities paragraph to a few lines of key details and choose some key achievements giving as much evidence and quantification as possible.

8.4.2 – Competences

Another well-used method is to start the CV with a list of your strong competences, in the form of short statements, still followed by the details of your employment with responsibilities and achievements, which could be like this (for the same person as in 8.4.1):

Financial experience: relevant experience running customer accounts functions, reducing debtor days/cash outstanding significantly.

Communication skills: outgoing personality with proven ability to improve relationships with customer accounts and sales teams, while successfully collecting debts

Leadership: recruiting and managing qualified/part-qualified team, recognised within BHP as the best-performing customer accounts team.

BHP Ltd	**Credit Controller**	**2002 - date**
CVA Ltd	**Credit Control Clerk**	**1998 - 2002**

You would include again details of responsibilities and achievements under each employer, altered so as not to duplicate the information set out in the competences.

8.4.3 – Skills summary

An alternative presentation within the jobs focus CV would be to have a summary of key skills at the top of the page (again, keep it to an important few – if you state that you have 20 key skills, it could give the impression that you are a generalist):

Key skills:
- Significantly reducing debtors - consistently
- Building and improving customer relationships
- Motivating department team

BHP Ltd   Credit Controller   2002 - date
Responsibilities: managing team of 12 qualified/part-qualified, to …
      [descriptive paragraph]
Achievements:
- Reducing outstanding debtors from x to y weeks (worth £XXX)
- Performance managing my team
- Improving customer relationships

CVA Ltd   Credit Control Clerk   1998 - 2002
Responsibilities:

8.4.4 – Functional

Where you have had a career which covers a number of aspects of a business, or in a particular functional area, you might want to consider a functional presentation. This can also be used if you lack a formal qualification but have wide experience in the functional area. This might come out as follows (for another finance person):

Management accounts   Within RJP, reorganising the department to reduce costs, while maintaining both morale and performance. Presenting accounts to the company management team monthly. Promoted on basis of performance in recruited role.

Credit control Promoted to managing bought ledger team, to reduce significant debtor backlog (successful). Joined as cashier, with significant prior experience, and later promoted to resolve problems in costing team.

Standard costing   Resolved personnel problems and introduced new costing system within budget and timescale.   [cont]

[cont]

RJP plc	**1996 - date**
Management accountant	2000-date
Accounts supervisor	1996-2000
Fisher Ltd	**1988 - 1996**
Bought ledger manager	1994-1996
Standard costing team	1990-1994
Senior cashiers clerk	1988-1990
Paykel Ltd	**1985-1988**
Cashier	

This presentation shows that although experience has been with only three companies (and doesn't make it obvious that the applicant has no accountancy qualifications) there is a fairly wide knowledge of the accounts function in a manufacturing environment and two companies have recruited and subsequently promoted the applicant.

8.4.5 – 'Bio' approach.

Sometimes, it may be appropriate to present a very short CV in the form of a 'third person summary' covering perhaps up to ½ page such as:

> Clive has an accountancy qualification (ACA) and has been with a number of well-known companies developing skills in credit control. He has worked in some tough commercial environments and would be an asset to any organisation seeking a radical improvement in its credit control processes and procedures.

This example is necessarily brief, but I'm sure it gives you the idea. This might be useful as an aid to networking or in job-search and job applications; it could help conceal age and lack of qualifications until the experience has been appreciated.

8.4.6 – Academic

Academic CVs seem to disobey many of the normal rules for commercial CVs – those judged to be good in academia are fairly long, have a lot of detail, and include long lists of publications. I have included a possible layout for an academic CV in Appendix I which is as follows (with a significant amount of text included under each of the bold headings):

Name
Current position
Department
Faculty
Educational qualifications (tertiary)

Previous appointments

Significant awards and distinctions

Professional societies etc

Invited seminars, talks, and conferences

Internal committees and teaching posts

Research specialities

Publications

Grants and funding obtained

8.5 – An objective?

Some commentators favour putting in a paragraph early in the CV defining your next career objective or the perceived next step for you. This can work well – someone looking for (say) a bought ledger supervisor is going to be attracted to a CV from an applicant which says 'Objective – bought ledger supervisor'.

Conversely, it can also work against you. If you have been a business development manager and see your next role as a business manager or managing director, and put this as your objective, you are likely to count yourself out of the running for a post as business development director of a larger or more complex business, which could provide an exciting challenge and become a very interesting job.

An objective does not appear on most people's CV, so if you decide to include one, make the inclusion work for you! Another useful way of focusing on this issue is to use the covering letter to make the point.

8.6 – A CV for interim

Many people consider becoming an interim manager when their career is interrupted by redundancy or some similar unexpected event. The attraction to interim work they feel is based on the concept (and other people's recommendations) that their experience will be put to good use temporarily while they look for a job. The reality is somewhat different. It's another competitive market – with many people looking for one of the few available assignments. So how do you 'score'?

First of all, you need to realise that this option is not seen by 'insiders' as a short-term option. It could turn out to be so, but the people recruiting interim managers will almost certainly want to see not only that you have relevant skills and experience but also that you are 'in it for the duration', i.e. you are there for (potentially) a long time. Interim work is too big a subject to cover here but, to succeed, you need to show a commitment to be in the interim market for (say) 3 to 5 years and set yourself up accordingly. If you are intending only to use interim work to 'fill the gap' until you find that desired permanent job, you'll need to explore how the market works to decide how best to market yourself while keeping your job-search options open.

I suggest that you repackage your CV to show from your experience to date (or perhaps within the last ten years) as many projects that look like a series of interim assignments as you can. Sure, you have been an employee whilst you carried them out, but how could you present the work you have done on a 'six-month-project' basis. The CV will need to show your full-time employed career, but should focus first on the interim elements. So perhaps one page of projects and then a second page of employment history.

8.7 – A CV for consultancy

Moving from employment to consultancy is often not the 'easy option' it is sometimes perceived to be. Consultancy is a whole new way of life, but friends and others may steer you towards this route if you are (say) over 40 and looking for a new role. The decision to 'go self-employed' has many implications, and you should consider it very carefully (and see my book *'Stop Dreaming & Start Doing'* for more information on this choice).

Whilst there is no requirement for a CV for people moving into consultancy, there is a real need to be able to show potential clients that you can do the sort of projects that you are now trying to sell. Again, it is a matter of viewing your experience from the 'consumer's end', i.e. your potential clients – and thinking about how you use that experience to demonstrate what you can do for them. It may be worth preparing a 'recent projects' sheet showing some projects that you have done which were of a consultancy nature for your former employers.

Chapter 8 – Key points

- Which style of CV is going to fit the roles that you will be seeking?

- What are your competitors using? Review any other CVs that you can obtain.

-

-

-

9

Putting It Together, Section by Section

9.1 – Introduction

Whatever you decide to do for the style of your CV, it's page one that sits on top and makes the first impression on the reader. A quick read through that first page must give the reader a convincing summary of your latest job, responsibilities, achievements, and what you can do for your reader. Bear this in mind as you develop your CV and its style.

In setting out the content of each section of the CV – I have used an order which is my preference, but don't feel constrained if you have a different preference; the words on content apply whatever the order you choose. There is some essential information which must be provided, even if in summary form, including contact details, organisations worked for, jobs/positions held, dates (full record), particulars of roles and achievements in each job, special skills, school and tertiary education (if any), and qualifications.

9.2 – Contact details

You may wonder why I say, 'You must put in your name, address and phone' – surely that's obvious? Well some people do get it wrong – like the client of mine without a job who didn't want his home phone number on his CV (he no longer had a work/mobile number) because he didn't want anyone to phone him at home (he felt work shouldn't interfere with home life). The net result was that head-hunters could not phone him and I think you have to be really special to require that people contact you by post!

Your address/phone/fax/mobile/email – your contact details – can be at the top of the first page of your CV, at the end of the last page, or as a header/footer on every page. None is uniquely correct, although most CVs will have all the contact details at the top of the first sheet. Include your usual postal address, phone number (mobile/cell phone), fax and email address (check that the email address sounds professional enough for you – not, for example, 'bigears@hotmail.com'). These details are less important than other information in creating a good impression, so they could be set in a slightly smaller typeface, or italic – as long as it is still legible.

Whatever else you do, put your name clearly and boldly at the top of the first sheet – it's important! You are the product, so tell them about it quickly! It's really not necessary to put all your names or initials, just what you are called. 'Is it Timothy or Tim?' can waste a couple of minutes, so if it's Tim, put Tim! However, if your name is John Jones, you may want to include a middle name/initial to create a distinction from other John Joneses. Put your name as a 'header' (or possibly 'footer') on every subsequent sheet in a smaller typeface, similar to the page numbering (e.g. Page 1 of 2) in case the sheets get separated.

Use only those degrees or qualifications after your name that are essential. A string of degrees, memberships and/or 'gongs' may not give the impression that you wish.

9.3 – Profile

If you are going to use one CV for all applications, you'll need to appeal to all sections of the community and so I'd recommend using a short profile of 3-6 lines. For a recruiter, the profile would ideally very short, factual, pithy and for a business person, perhaps somewhat longer, punchy, full and effective. So you'll need to seek a compromise.

In writing a profile, you're looking to provide the reader with a sharp and positive description of who you are, what you do, and how you can improve the reader's business. I think of it in terms of preparing a 30 second statement that you would be comfortable (well almost comfortable!) saying – if you had only those 30 seconds to leave the right impression. This is sometimes called 'the elevator pitch' – your chance to tell someone everything they need to know about you in the time it takes for the elevator to go from floor x to floor y.

You do not want trite, hackneyed, or tired words and phrases, nor do you want to sound self-congratulatory. Use facts, not subjective claims, and ask yourself 'Who says?' about all such statements. Avoid making general statements which cannot be proved – try to be specific, even if it's 'regularly beating tough sales targets' and be prepared to explain and evidence this later in your interview.

A couple of examples of profiles:

Professional Real Estate executive with experience across a wide range of sectors and geographical regions. Has delivered significant change programmes throughout Europe, Middle East, Asia & the Americas in retail, office & manufacturing. Enhancing value at the same time as significantly reducing costs and improving customer service.

Experienced, well-qualified medical practitioner with wide clinical knowledge of health promotion, primary care and general practice, acute care, emergency care, and hospital care. Secure research background in public health and community medicine.

9.4 – Skills/Competences

Other key information that you need to include in the opening paragraphs of your CV is a summary of your main skills and competences. Given that you have limited space, a long profile will require a short skills summary – or vice-versa. A short focused list of key skills can be very persuasive – provided that they match up with you, the job, and are what you talk about at interview!

There are broadly two ways of listing your skills in your CV. Firstly, if you want to combine the listing with a profile, then the skills summary needs to be fairly short – in order to ensure that your contact details + profile + key skills are within the first half page, allowing your most recent job to cover the second half of page one. In this case, give perhaps 4-6 key skills such as:

- Strong communication skills
- Negotiating and persuading
- Resilient and determined
- Setting and meeting tough goals
- Recruiting and developing key staff

Alternatively, the listing of your skills can take up more space or could be phrased as competence statements (see 8.4.2) which can then replace the profile, e.g.:

Strong communication skills: strong oral and written communication skills in marketing liaison and in staff management, generating improved performance in both areas.

Setting and meeting tough goals: regularly setting tough business targets with proven performance both in sales and profitability levels. Launching new brands in company record timescales with long-term regular market share gains.

9.5 – Career history

This is one of the main sections of the CV for most people. There are a number of combinations of how you can present your career history in order to bring out the information on which you wish to focus. Whatever style of presentation you choose, you should set out your career in reverse chronological order (i.e. the most recent role first), with a full history of your employment, giving less and less detailed information as you go back further into the past.

Use the same paragraph style for detailing all jobs, for all employers and so on, as this adds to the clarity of presentation. So, perhaps each employment section could start with the employer's name in bold type, followed by the job title, with the dates of employment (start/finish) on the right hand side of the page. (NB the dates should be complete, without any gaps, and in most cases, the year alone, not month/year, is sufficient detail.).

Group the information about each job together, with smaller spaces between the paragraphs within the section; allow larger spaces between jobs, to focus the reader on each 'packet' of related information.

If (some of) the employers are not generally well known, you can consider including a short description of the employer's business. The only purpose of this is to help sell you, not to educate the world in the business of your former employers, so keep it short and to the point (it's using up space that you could use to talk about you).

If you want to draw attention to the key organisations and roles you have had in your career to date, you could start with a summary on page one thus:

Employer A Ltd	**Job title**	**2001-2005**
Employer B plc	**Job title**	**1996-2001**
Employer C Ltd	**Job title**	**1992-1996**

This focuses the reader on these key names and dates before getting into the details of each job.

Alternatively, you may not want to highlight that you've been with one employer for the last 25 years. In this case, I'd suggest you do not start with …

Employer A Ltd	**1979-2004**

… but instead list out each role to show the scale of each, the variety etc and, if possible, the differences between the various jobs and your career progression, or show your competences in extended format.

With each role, you should define your responsibilities and achievements (unless the responsibilities are self-evident) possibly using the following layout:

9.5.1 – Responsibilities

Responsibilities are different from achievements. Responsibilities are those matters under your management or control, which would also have been the responsibility of anyone else doing the same job at that time. Responsibilities do not, on their own, deliver results or change. Spend less time/space within your CV setting out your responsibilities than on your achievements, but do try to put numbers or values to them where possible. I suggest you limit the space spent on responsibilities to 2-4 lines as they are not unique to you.

9.5.2 – Achievements

These are the things you did where you made a difference. You must describe in your marketing document (your CV) how you changed, stopped, started, or completed something. Quantify and qualify these achievements wherever possible. Make them sound interesting – so that you get asked about them in the interview. Don't give all the details – otherwise there'll be little reason to call you in or to ask you about when you get there (and you'll run out of space in your CV). Achievements will show how you can make a difference for your new employer.

9.5.3 – Skills and skill stories

'Skill stories' are what I call the 'colour pictures' that make you stand out. Prepare some notes on your achievements to describe what happened and include the key details. In writing about your achievements in your CV, make sure that you include a few 'leads' into your skill stories. You want the reader of your CV to ask you questions about some of the things you have done – so 'set them up' in the achievements sections. What could be more natural for an interviewer than to say 'You said here that you ... – tell me about it.'

9.6 – **Previous career** (for students and college leavers)

When you have only recently left school or college, it's just not possible to show a long career with many responsibilities and achievements. Employers do recognise this situation and are looking for how you address their concerns about your attitude to work, your experience of work, responsibility and so on.

Review your life so far and consider how to include any experience which shows you have had responsibility for people, cash, achieving results and such like. It could be for example that you managed a short project at school/university to promote something, worked in a shop during the holidays, raised money for a charity, or enjoyed some work experience (and can talk about it). Look at some of the sample CVs and think back – have you done anything like the examples quoted. I have yet to work with a college leaver who has no relevant experience for the world of work.

9.7 – **Previous career** (for mature employees)

If your career stretches back for, say, 20 years or more, remember that the potential employer is more interested in the detail of the most recent ten or twelve years of your business or commercial life. You should consider consolidating the prior experience into a short paragraph highlighting the relevant overall experience, progression and so on.

It is probably not essential at this stage for you to list out all of your early employers or to set out full dates of each job – just as long as there are not any gaps in the dates that you include that will attract attention. If you decide to summarise, try to focus the reader on the points that will add to your current career.

9.8 – Education

If you are in, or heading for, business life, most readers of your CV will be interested in the commercial experience that you've had before they look to see what academic background you had earlier to support it. If you so choose, you can include the complete details of your education but the space is probably better utilised focussing on your career experience. Include the schools/institutions where you studied, together with the dates, and your highest level qualifications (on the basis that if you achieved 'A' levels, you must have GCSEs). You can, of course, include summary information of the intermediate academic achievements if it is important to you, but if it is a long time ago, it's unlikely to turn heads now.

If you are in academia, it is likely that people will still be more keen to review what you have done recently before looking at your earlier education, but the latter is possibly higher up the scale of interest than for business people. Generally, you have more space in an academic CV, so you can include more details of earlier education.

'Other training' is often included in the education section. If you have undertaken some relevant courses or training, then list out the most important. However, don't include every single one-day course that you've been on – it probably makes you sound desperate – or a perennial student!

9.9 – Other interests

When you have completed the review of your career, it can be useful to include some 'other interests', i.e. what you do in your non-work or spare time. Some of my clients will argue that this is unnecessary, but it does add a little character to what can be otherwise a fairly 'businessy' CV. It may also be useful in a 'bonding process' when you and the interviewer find you have similar interests.

More useful however, is when your non-work activities reveal something about you or add to the picture you have been building in your work roles – such as being a leader, or working in a team to change things. Make sure that the other interests say something positive about you however – 'watching TV', 'socialising', or 'eating out', hardly conjure up a positive image in the mind of the reader.

9.10 – Bio details

In some countries, it is no longer required (or even legal) to require you to include in your CV personal details such as your age/dob, marital status, ethnicity or religion. Of these, currently in the UK only the age/dob is expected, but I always suggest putting it near the end. In writing the opening profile, you are looking to provide the reader with a short, sharp, image of you to 'colour' the rest of his reading. I've suggested that you lead off with your most recent experience, written in a way to impress and interest the reader. By the time he gets to the end of the CV, his impression is probably pretty well formed and (we hope!) he is enthused by you – at which point your age will matter less.

Do keep these bio details relevant – e.g. if you are a truck driver, then an HGV licence is relevant; it is probably not so important if you are a sales manager (even if it may be useful). I have often seen 'Clean driving licence' on a senior manager's CV – which is usually unnecessary.

9.11 – Publications

If you are pursuing an academic career (or even if you are not and you have an impressive list of publications), show these in an appendix to your CV, not in the CV itself, again listing the most recent ones first. Prepare your lists of publications in the order where you are sole author, lead author, joint author and so on as your role becomes less and less important.

Chapter 9 – Key points

- Clear, separate, sections of the CV will help the reader to pick up relevant and related information.

- The information does not have to be total and complete – you are trying to interest not submerse the reader. Pick out the highlights, the key facts etc. which will influence and impress.

-

-

-

10

Issues

10.1 – Introduction

I know that sometimes we can all think that the perceived 'rules' of CV writing do not to apply to our own CV, or there are things to include or exclude that escape the normal rules. This chapter is about those items. Rest assured – you are very unlikely indeed to be the only person who has had the particular 'problem' that you are keen to address. It really is important that you do not lie in your CV, nor should you be 'economical with the truth' about anything; it is however possible to focus the reader's attention on what really matters.

Taking as an example a fairly uncommon occurrence, it's not really relevant or useful to set out in your CV the details of how the company employing you went into receivership – what is more important is that you know why it happened and how to avoid it in future, as well as all the good things you did to bring such success as the company did have. After such an experience you may be a much better bet for employment than someone who has never even come near such a significant problem. So, include the role in your CV, your achievements with that company, the effect that you had to minimise the risks and problems – and be prepared to talk about it all, including the receivership, at interview.

10.2 – Job-hopping

Swift changes of job happen – to some people, some times. It can be due to their own mistakes, company mistakes, economic conditions, or just 'happenstance'. Some observers would view a job change every two years as job-hopping; others would see it as the way to get on in their industry. These days, one job lasting only 3 to 9 months is explainable – several jobs consecutively, each lasting only 3 to 9 months, will be harder to justify.

It is also broadly accepted that you can move employer and/or job about every two to three years as part of an active career management programme. This is fine, but what do you do if you have had several jobs of shorter duration?

If you have had a number of short-term roles in one firm, it may indeed work in your favour as it can show that you have been regularly moved as a rising star to assist the organisation deal with problem areas or to take advantage of opportunities. If this is the case, make reference to it in your CV, using words like 'requested to move to new role to ...' or 'moved to ... to take advantage of ...' or 'to create, resolve ...'

Alternatively, you may have had several short-term jobs, with different employers, in a short period, which would not look good on your CV. There is no simple solution to this. If the jobs were a long time ago, it may look better if you consolidate the jobs into a separate section starting with the words 'Various short term roles to gain experience of ...' If it is more recent, it may be more appropriate to explain that the market was in recession and everyone was retrenching, or the particular problems that befell the organisation. I would normally advise against putting in the reason for leaving (unless a promotion), but in this case it may be the only way to cover the apparent instability.

This really is an area where it can be very useful to talk over your thoughts on presentation with your coach, with colleagues, or possibly even with a friendly recruiter.

10.3 – Gaps

Readers of CVs tend to be suspicious of gaps and make their own assessment of the reasons – which may be totally unjustified – so don't leave any gaps! Gaps of a few months between jobs can be expected and should not be hidden from view, although if you are not using the month/year format to show the period of employment, such gaps may not show up immediately. There is certainly no need to highlight such gaps in your CV – you can decide how to talk about them at interview – e.g. what did you do with your time whilst unemployed?

If you spent a year travelling around the world – what is the best way of presenting it? Was it self-funded or sponsored? What did you learn? Was it purely holiday? If you had a gap during which you studied, say what you did, why, and what the result was. If you undertook some charitable work, say what your role was, and how successful it was.

10.4 – Short-term projects

Sometimes people take on short-term projects when they are between jobs, either as consultants, or as interim managers, or simply to help out a friend with a business problem. If this type of project is part of your normal work, think about how best to present this to your (potential) next employer. If it's not relevant to your work, could you – or how could you – make it so? At the most basic level, it could be that you undertook the work to earn money to enable you to start/finish a project. Alternatively, it might provide you with project management or leadership experience, or the chance to use newly acquired financial skills.

10.5 – Oddball or wacky CVs

You might think about attracting attention by producing a 'seriously different' CV. True, most CVs in the market are similar in many ways, and you really do want yours to stand out. However, most people reading CVs are mature, sensible business people and whilst you want to attract their attention, it needs to be done in the right way. You certainly could (for example) print your CV on fluorescent orange paper – it would get noticed, but unless that was very relevant to the job for which you are applying, it's more than likely to earmark your CV to go straight in the bin.

It is still possible to bring in some new ideas to your CV, but they need to be very relevant to your career, your job and you. So if you are a professional in marketing, you will be judged by the professional nature of your own key marketing document. If you are a graphic designer, your CV will need to be particularly well laid out. And if you say that one of your key skills is communication, then the CV had better be pretty good at telling the world effectively about you and generating a high degree of retained interest!

10.6 – Living overseas and job-hunting here

I have worked with a number of clients over the years who have been laid off by their employers from an overseas job, or who have taken a redundancy package there, and who have then sought to get a job 'back home'. I don't intend to go into job-searching techniques here, except to say that if you want to job-search in the UK, then having a UK address on your CV is almost essential.

Other people must be able to judge that you are able to travel to your job-search environment fairly easily and most reviewers will look at your address and assess the likelihood (in their view) of your doing so. You may be very prepared to travel nationally or internationally for interview (or for a job) but it is their view that is significant. Most employers and often most recruiters will be unenthusiastic about a CV which says you wish to move, for example, to London from Dallas, Texas.

If you are living in Japan (or Newcastle) and job-searching in London, you really need a London address from which to be seen to operate. If that is not your home, then the best route is probably to have a friend/relation who will allow you to use their address and who will review and forward your mail – but you may need to rent a local forwarding address/phone.

10.7 – Technical terms, 'buzzwords' and clichés

It's very tempting to use 'standard industry' language or technical terms when preparing your CV and all I can say is 'Don't'. Many readers of your CV will not be as experienced in the industry as you and if they are constantly stopping to wonder at the meaning of a word or phrase, they will lose focus on you and your skills. As an example, most people would understand Windows as an operating system for PCs, and some might recognise what VMS, Unix and Linux refer to, but how many would know what PAWZ, DECPS, VPA, SPM Best/1 and Predict are? Try to keep it simple and save the technical terms for when you need them.

'Buzzwords' and clichés are usually a definite 'No thank you' for a CV. Again, you are seeking to impress with your communication skills, to be interesting, and to appear to be someone who will make a positive difference to a business. The language you use can help or hinder you in making this impression. See Appendix II for some expressions you might want to avoid.

10.8 – The 'I' word

'I' is the shortest word in the dictionary and draws attention to itself on the page – as a very lonely letter. If you are writing in the first person – and if you can possibly do so, consider different sentence constructions and abbreviations to avoid using 'I's. If you use 'short form sentences' (e.g. 'Creating new business opportunities') the 'I' naturally drops out of use and the sentence becomes more interesting and informative as a result – as well as being more 'catchy'. On other occasions, you may want to use the past tense (e.g. 'Created new business opportunities') –

perhaps to emphasise completion of projects.

There may be other occasions when it will be appropriate to write in the third person, although it's not generally my favourite style ('John is an experienced professional general manager, with ...').

10.9 – Too young/inexperienced

Sometimes you see a role that would be fantastic for you – but they are looking for someone who's a little older or who has greater and more demonstrable experience. You cannot lie about what you have done, but you can put forward your relevant experience in as positive a light as possible, you can demonstrate your enthusiasm, and you can research deeply before you apply to see what you can do to 'catch up' If the employer is rigidly set in his ideas, then there will be little you can do – but if there is any possibility of your experience being of interest, how can you build a picture of you being a suitable 'young challenger'?

10.10 – Too old

Even though employers should not preclude older applicants, there is a 'youth culture' and advertisements sometimes make it pretty clear that there is an age limitation. Often however, the strongest constraint for someone who is older than the advertiser's specified requirement is in the mind of the applicant himself. There is no reason why you cannot present yourself as suitable – unless the employer really is prejudiced. Try to be seen as someone who is the right age – but with 10 years' more experience! And – put your age at the end of your impressive CV, so that readers are thoroughly impressed with you before they get to the date of birth.

Alternatively, sometimes you may be able to approach the employer with a longer, but very well thought out, letter of application showing how you meet the bill but without the age details (in the first instance). However, this is unlikely to work well if a recruiter asks you to send your CV!

10.11 – Too good/experienced

I have had clients who have wanted to move down the employment ladder to more junior positions because they have had a bad experience, or they have been searching for some time and feel that they will stand a better chance of applying for a job where they are well over-skilled. It doesn't really work – the employer is left wondering why. If the applicant is so well qualified, why will this lesser role be satisfactory? Will he stay? It can be done, but your CV is unlikely to help and it's impossible to lie about your seniority. Yes, it is possible to 'play down' the past roles, but only by so much. If this really is your objective, you stand a much greater chance of realising it by using your personal network to find a new role than by applying blind to an advertisement.

10.12 – Conspicuous lack of success in last job

If your last role really did not work out, for whatever reason, I would still suggest that if at all possible, you prepare your CV on the basis of your achievements. It's far better to talk through your reason for leaving or a lack of success on a face-to-face basis than to try it on paper – where you may just be making it easy for the reader to say 'Not this one'. I've worked with people at all levels who have left companies in apparent disaster scenarios – and in nearly all cases the client has been able to come up with a positive CV.

10.13 – Prejudice

Particularly in view of relevant legislation, you should be very unlikely to come across blatant prejudice against gender, religion, race or ethnic origin, etc. If you do, whilst the law is on your side, it may not be the most sensible thing for you to pursue at that time. If your prime purpose is to get yourself employed, a major campaign deviation to pursue legally a prejudice case may (unfortunately) be too expensive in the use of your precious time and cash.

A better approach would be to seek out actively other target organisations in the sector (and there are a lot of them) where such prejudice is not in evidence.

Chapter 10 – Key points

- **Issues should not be avoided – but should be presented in the best possible and honest light.**

- **Try not to use the word 'I'.**

-

-

-

11

Add-ons

11.1 – Introduction

I'm assuming at this point that you've been preparing all the information for your CV along the lines suggested but there are a couple of items where any relevant presentation will be far too long for my 'two pages' guide. What do you do?

11.2 – Publications

The theme that a CV should be about two pages long really is an 'industry standard'. However, if you are an academic, one of the key criteria will be your list of publications – which should be attached to the first CV you submit to a possible employer.

The rules for presenting publications in academic CVs are much the same as for listing them in any publication for a respected industry journal. Many such journals have websites telling you how to present your prior publications if you are submitting a paper and I would suggest that you look in one or two high quality journals in your profession to establish the publication criteria. These may be listed under 'Guidance for authors' or similar, and you are likely to be asked to list the most recent and the most important of your publications first, i.e. sole or lead authorships will come first in the list, then joint authorships, and later listing those where you only had a minor role. This can and should be presented separately as an appendix to the main CV – even if it is not headed as an appendix.

11.3 – Presentations

You may have other materials that you wish to show to your potential employer – perhaps a PowerPoint presentation or details of projects you have managed, a portfolio of designs, or photographs of buildings you have designed/erected/managed etc. Usually it's not going to be appropriate to include these with your CV as an initial document (unless of course you have something like the design of the Sydney Opera House or the Guggenheim Museum to your name – in which case ignore this advice!)

It may however be relevant to mention something in the letter that accompanies your CV and certainly you will want to make sure that you have everything in order so that you can, at moment's notice, talk it through with someone at a meeting or interview. You may also want to take it along with you to any interview – but be sure it's relevant. It can be difficult to stop someone who is determined to show you a project completed 20 years ago – which does nothing to build a good impression with the interviewer who is under some time pressure!

Chapter 11 – Key points

- Keep the CV short and to the point and relegate other vitally important information to an appendix.

- Other relevant information or presentations – be prepared to take them along to interview.

-

-

-

12

'No-nos, Cultural Differences or New Ideas?

12.1 – Introduction

This chapter includes the tips that I couldn't get to fit elsewhere!

12.2 – Other ideas

Photographs

I'm sometimes asked 'What about putting my photograph on my CV?' The unfortunate truth is that it's more likely to work against you, than for you – in the UK. I've not yet met a recruiter in the UK who has expressed any interest in a photo accompanying a CV although I believe, from French colleagues, that it is fairly common to add a photo to your CV in France – so local knowledge on this issue is important. The current view in UK however is 'no photographs'. Most of us do not have the film-star looks that will appeal and although there is some evidence that 'good looks' do count in the recruitment process – why put the reader off at an early stage! If you do need a photograph for something, get a professional photographer involved. I have seen some pretty awful 'snaps' which would put off even the applicant's own mother!

Videos, CDs, or DVDs

What about including your CV on a CD or video? Broadly the same applies as with photographs. If you can get someone to sit down and watch your video/CD/DVD, and if the work on the video clip is very professionally done, then you are likely to present a more complete picture of you than is possible on paper and you'll possibly capture the reader's attention for a longer spell. Again, the unusual is probably not a good idea (unless it is part of your job to prepare such things) and I would still suggest sticking with the standard hard-copy CV for nearly all situations.

Salary

Should you include salary details or not in your CV? Unless you are specifically asked to include this information when you respond to an advertisement, a letter or a phone call, don't include your salary the first time you write. If you are asked to include this information, put it in your covering letter not in the CV. Remember that you have some flexibility in the numbers you quote – the range goes from your basic salary to the total value of your remuneration package. So, if you are concerned that the last overall package you received was higher than you can expect currently in the market, you can always say 'I'm seeking something around my present salary of £xx' without specifying the total package. If on the other hand you are looking at a role which is significantly larger than your last job, but one you feel you can do, you can say 'I'm looking to improve on my present package of £xx'.

Hackneyed phrases

Try to avoid 'business-speak' in anything you produce – your CV, your letter, and in your interview responses. There are still far too many CVs around full of words like:

- ✗ Blue-sky thinking
- ✗ 24/7
- ✗ Ballpark
- ✗ Value-add
- ✗ Leverage

I think that these should be avoided in any conversation – spoken or written – and I've set out a few of my pet 'hates' in Appendix II.

12.3 – Professional CV writers

No book on CVs would be complete without a comment on the various people who can help you to write your CV – or others who will write it for you. I'm going to stick to these two categories for my comments. I know from experience that having someone else help with preparing your CV can be invaluable. A fresh pair of eyes, a serious challenge to some of your comments, a searching review with you of your career, and a comparison of you and your career with your CV, can all make a world of difference to the quality of the final document. Use your coach, a colleague, or a friend to help you do this.

I'm much less enthusiastic about the second category – the professional CV writer – someone who takes your information and prepares a CV for you to use. I include in this the standard templates supplied with PC software packages from well-known computer software companies. It seems to me that such a CV is unlikely to be 'you' – it's someone else's reflection on you, and therefore it is likely to be less influential than your own work. That's not to say you can't learn anything from such help – but I'd suggest that if you do engage such a writer, you then take the document produced and turn it into your own document – one that you feel comfortable using in the market.

Chapter 12 – Key points

- Keep your CV as professional as you are.
- Don't forget the true purposes of a CV.
-
-
-

13

Summary

13.1 – Introduction

You should by now have a pretty good idea of how you want your CV to look and 'feel' – but just in case, here's a summary of the key points to remember.

 Chapter 13 – Key points

- First and foremost, you want your CV to attract attention for the right reasons and persuade someone to want to meet you. It's about effective marketing of you.

- The CV must appeal to all sections of your reading audience – whether employers, friends, or recruitment agents. It must also attract those you do not know.

- Your CV needs to specify clearly your skills and positive attributes, your relevant experience and training, and any other relevant points, in a way that attracts the reader's attention.

- You are operating in a competitive market – anything less than your best will not do.

- Get advice and ideas from other people, other CVs, recruiters, indeed from anywhere! Sift out and apply the best advice.

- Being over-modest is not a good approach. Exhibit due pride in your achievements and skills.

- Spend time collecting information on your career, your achievements, your outside interests and anything else you might need for your CV and interviews. Check the information and get it consistent. Analyse it all carefully and consider how best to present it to market and sell you.

- Choose your presentation carefully (see Chapter 6 'The Basic Rules' for detail comments). In particular focus on content first, style second, and length third, and remember to impress by being brief.

- Make sure the CV looks interesting, is easy and relevant to read, and conveys the key messages that you want – in 90 seconds.

-

-

-

APPENDIX I

Sample CVs

- The following CVs are included not because they are brilliant and should be copied, but to show you some differing styles and ways of presenting people. They are to give you ideas, for you to critique – and review the commentaries I've provided for each.

- CVs such as these samples should be produced on A4 stationery – the ones shown here are (obviously!) photo-reduced to fit the smaller A5 page.

- In most cases, the outside, single-line box would not be used on an A4 sheet, and margins would be 20-25mm.

Commentary

The first CV (overleaf) shows the use of profile and key skills sections. James wanted to draw attention to his rise from auditing through finance, sales and marketing to business management. So the first page lists his employers (the employers' real names were well known) and his roles without details. The second page then lists out key achievements in each of the recent roles. He has a number of points of interest for the interviewer to explore – e.g. the Disease State Management and 'Business Partners for Results' programmes as well as identifiable achievements (sales up 11% – above market average) – and Fulham Football Club! In mentioning his family, he decided not to highlight the fact that he was divorced at the CV stage.

CV 1 – A senior manager's CV

JAMES MISCELL

25 Bakewell Avenue, London SE10 2EB
Tel: +44 (0)20 8883 1234 Mob: +44 (0) 7736 102 102
Email: jmiscell@hotmail.com

Innovative, results-driven and customer-focused commercial executive with proven expertise in finance and marketing, international experience and leadership ability. Key abilities include:

- Developing business strategy, analysis, and planning
- Having the vision and effecting business change
- Setting and meeting tough business goals
- Negotiating and persuading
- Independent and creative thinking, but team player
- Developing high calibre people
- Tough-minded, determined, and resilient

CAREER SUMMARY

PHARMACEUT UK   **2002 - 2005**

Business Director
Head of Sales and Marketing. Sales £80m, expenditure £25m, staff 160

AMERICEX UK   **1997 - 2002**

Sales & Marketing Director
Sales £35m, expenditure £8m, staff 100
Finance Director & Company Secretary
Price and product negotiations, reducing operating costs, 35 staff including IT and Admin

PIPERCAN INTERNATIONAL   **1997**

Business Director
Head of Sales and Marketing. Sales £80m, expenditure £25m, staff 160

AMERICEX CORPORATION   **1989 - 1996**

International Controller, Animal Health Division
Manager Financial Analysis & Planning for US subsidiary California. Sales $500m
Manager Corporate Audit Services California
UK Financial Accounting Manager
Internal Auditor

INDEX

Inventory Accountant   **1987 - 1988**

BAKER & MASON

Internal Auditor   **1986 - 1987**

NATIONAL AUDIT OFFICE

Auditor   **1981 - 1986**

MAJOR BUSINESS ACHIEVEMENTS (1997 – 2005)

2004-5 Pharmaceut UK	- Regionalised UK company commercial operations to meet changing customer needs - Successfully launched new AIDS drug
2003-4 Pharmaceut UK	- Developed Disease State Management initiatives to put company at forefront in key therapeutic areas - Upgraded strategic planning process
2002-3 Pharmaceut UK	- Integrated commercial operations following takeover. Delivered sales/profit targets throughout integration - Reduced combined cost base by £5m (20%) - Grew UK sales by 11% versus 8% market growth
2001-2 Americex UK	- Grew UK sales by 10% in first year (best since 1992) - Grew export sales by 50% and profits by 100% within two years - Introduced integrated sales/marketing business planning - Introduced 'one team exceeding customer expectations' programme
2001 Americex UK	- Negotiated sale of declining product to competitor for $1m
1997-2000 Americex UK	- Negotiated five price increases worth more than £1m pa with Dept of Health in tough circumstances - Negotiated commercial aspects of two product co-promotion contracts, one product in-licensing contract and one product out-licensing contract - Introduced value-added and activity-based costing concepts and reduced operating costs by over 10% (£1m) - Introduced successful customer focus programme into department "Business Partners for Results"

EDUCATION

ACCA qualified
Diploma in Accounting and Auditing (1st place) – Westminster University
3 'A' levels, 11 'O' levels

PROFESSIONAL BODIES

Fellow Association of Chartered Certified Accountants (FCCA)
Member Institute of Directors
Member Institute of Management

PERSONAL

Dob 30 March 1963
Two children
Leisure activities – Health club (4x per week), Member Fulham FC Managers Club, Business magazines

CV 2 – A 'functional' CV for a senior manager

Trevor Parker

110 Drewett Street, Birmingham B42 7EY
Tel: 0121 496 4823   Mob: 07958 506 132
Email: trevorparker@yahoo.com

Commercial manager with proven record of meeting and beating corporate objectives through leadership, planning and organisation abilities. Key experience:

- Leading/motivating regional team (45) in demanding retail environment and regularly beating tough business targets
- Recruiting, training and developing key staff, improving business performance through team efforts
- Clear and effective communication with departmental, company, and external staff
- Agreeing targets with team for new business and ensuring sales and profit targets met
- Developing business and financial plans with team to ensure regular success. Managing departmental budget.

COMPETENCES

Leadership

Described in 360 appraisals as an "excellent leader who motivates his team" using strong interpersonal skills and delegating management style. Introduced personal development plans for whole team, resulting in significant and measurable improvement in motivation and performance. Built team by recruitment and development to become the #1 performing division in company in 2003 and 2004. Seen as a coach for other divisions by Board.

Planning and Controlling

Wide knowledge of project management techniques and use of management accounts for control purposes. Running complex company-critical projects, giving experience of crisis management, attention to detail, and managing team through periods of low morale, when differing management styles were required. Innovating as needed to bring difficult projects forward and hit targets. Creating local and business plans for 1-36 mth projects. Managing factory closure, with minimal loss of production and maintained workforce relations.

Organising

Managing own department, working with other company departments, and with external partners (clients, franchisees, and suppliers) to achieve company goals. Regularly leading discussions on corporate communications to ensure objectives met in the most efficient manner. Leading discussions within professional body to engage all members in future association plans. Successfully running national conferences (7 years).

1 of 2

EMPLOYMENT

Regional Sales Manager	Beautyshop plc	1994 – 2005
Area Sales Manager	Beautyshop plc	1987 – 1994
Area Sales Manager	DSE Electronics plc	1984 – 1987
Sales Manager	DDL plc	1974 – 1984
Sales Executive	Elite Copiers plc	1968 – 1974

EDUCATION

1 'A' levels, 6 'O' levels

PERSONAL & INTERESTS

Dob 30 March 1950
Two adult children
Other interests: Past Chair of area Institute of Sales and Marketing, tennis (club captain twice), recently taken up skiing.

Commentary

The CV that follows is for Trevor, an older client, who was made redundant when his employer was acquired. He initially felt he would never get another job, especially in sales. His CV promotes his general business skills, with strong reference to sales and retail experience – so that he could be considered for other positions. He has not moved around much, so the CV emphasises the three main competence areas. Pastimes (tennis and skiing) indicate that he is very active and that he's not ready yet for retirement. Having been chairman of his local area institute and club captain says something about his leadership ability.

CV3 – A banker's CV

IAN RICHARDSON

20 Cromwell Road, London W4 2EB
Tel: 020 7632 4327   Mob: 07748 560562
Email: imrichardson@hotmail.com

Banking director

1996 – date   **Megabank Group**
Director
Director four subsidiary companies

Completed strategic review of:

- Information infrastructure for corporate finance front office
- Internal communication systems in investment bank
- Management accounting methods
- Involvement in all parts of Asia-Pacific region, especially Japan

Managed international software development project to establish group-wide system for generating and maintaining corporate finance marketing materials.

Key member of financial structuring team which developed a series of hybrid equity and tax-based transactions exceeding £2bn in value over 3 years

- Convertible Capital Bonds (*selection of companies involved listed*)
- Europreference Shares (*selection of companies involved listed*)
- Exchangeable Bonds (*selection of companies involved listed*)
- Corporate financial restructurings (*selection of companies involved listed*)
- Lease-based subordinated financings (*selection of companies involved listed*)

1989 – 1996   **Morning Herald**
Head 'The Daily Financial' column

Successfully trained and managed inexperienced team. Grew and maintained reputation of column as the City's leading commentary. Awarded *James Windsor Memorial Prize* in 1993

Leading feature writer on financial markets, corporate events, and industrial developments.

Joined as Economics Correspondent and promoted to member of financial writing team in 1991 and Head in 1994

1987 – 1989   **NEDO**
Staff Economist

Personal
1987   B Phil Kings College Cambridge
1980-83   BA (First) in PPE, Kings College Cambridge Open Scholar
1984-85   Yale University Kennedy Scholar
1971-79   Reyton College

Interests   Pianist, gardener and cook. Enjoys cricket in summer, squash in winter. Voracious reader

FINANCING PROJECTS

June '02	Capital raising for Megabank Group (subordinated convertible issue)	Reconciled numerous objectives Group -- not all finally required: "Core" capital status of instrument; creation of new class of equity capital; equity treatment in balance sheet; tax deductibility; timing; pricing.
July '00	Exchangeable bond issue for [major listed plc] £500k NPV	£450m raised; X plc's stake in Y plc neutralised; cooperation in development of Yplc's fields in North Sea underpinned
Feb '00	Subordinated debt for Y plc £250k NPV	Designed structure to enable Yplc to raise preference share capital using back-to-back structure to exploit capacity in UK banks for risk-free franked income and in Japan for subordinated debt
	[Ian then listed a full page of financing projects in his CV]	

STRATEGY PROJECTS

April '04	Review management accounting methods Intangible benefit	Devised model to extract early warning indicators from accounting data that had previously not been used for any "management" purpose.
Jan 04	Review of internal communications in the investment bank Intangible benefit	Structural weaknesses identified, short and long term remedies recommended
Nov '03	Study of the information infrastructure for Megabank corporate finance Benefit £1m pa = £7m (NPV)	Detailed recommendations leading (on full implementation) to savings of £1m per year in occupancy costs alone. Most recommendations currently in progress.
	[Ian then set out a full page of strategic projects in his CV]	

Commentary

Ian has provided a pithy one-page summary of his career, an interesting mix of financial journalism and then corporate finance and banking. He has supported this summary with two appendices showing summary details of the projects he has managed or carried out – separated into financing and strategy projects.

CV 4 – PA or secretary's CV

Emily Nicholls

9 Park Close, London N20 0DJ
Tel: 020 8368 1963   Mob: 07881 191 931
Email: ENichols21@hotmail.com

Experienced, professional, and well-organised PA/Secretary. Good administration skills. Flexible, loyal and provides conscientious support to manager and team.

Key skills:

- Efficient and well-organised, able to prioritise and deliver on time
- Experience at senior level in a sales environment
- Able to switch priorities to meet demands in a pressurised role
- Supportive team member

CAREER SUMMARY

DENISON EUROPE Ltd   **2000 – 2005**

PA and Administration Coordinator
Confidential support to Area Sales Director, management team, and other managers

- Organising and hosting overseas customer visits, promoting corporate image
- Delivering marketing reports on-time
- Planning and organising conferences and events
- Diary management for department, administration of budgets, expenses, and sales details for incentive scheme
- Support as required for finance and HR departments

Page 1 of 2

NOREX LONDON   1994 – 2000

Administrator/Secretary
Secretarial support to General Manager and team, together with collating information for accounts. Event organising, travel management, and departmental budget administration
- Restored and then maintained excellent working relationships within department and team.
- Improved reporting times by reorganising information flow and content
- Organised and ran several sales conferences successfully

Career break   1990 – 1994
Raising family

Benecom Travel
Starting as a telemarketer, promoted to team leader and then to MD's secretary. Overachieving monthly sales targets regularly in telesales led to promotion.

Prior experience
On leaving school and secretarial course, undertook various temporary roles from 1988 – 1990 to gain experience in the commercial world.

EDUCATION AND TRAINING

Pitman typing, Pitman shorthand (80 wpm)

5 CSEs 2 GCEs
Microsoft – Word, Excel, PowerPoint, Access, Outlook

PERSONAL

Dob 23.06.70
Married, two children (13 and 10)
Full clean driving licence, own car.

Commentary

Emily not only has skills as a PA/Secretary, but also in telesales. Although she took time out with a young family (and it is much better to clarify this than leave a gap), she has clearly organised her domestic life now to permit holding a responsible job.

CV 5 – Finance manager's CV

Rod Witherspoon

71 Hancock Drive, Stanmore, Mddx HA7 3PH
Tel: 020 8934 5564   Mob: 07747 931 920
Email: randjwitherspoon@btinternet.com

Commercially aware finance manager with good communication skills developed over a broad range of industries. An effective team leader committed to contributing to corporate objectives.

Key skills:

- Provider of timely financial information including US reporting
- Constructive interaction with Marketing/Sales/Production personnel
- Team recruitment, motivation, development.

CAREER

McQUARIE (PsiMedica division)   **1998 – 2005**
Distribution of orthopaedic products to NHS/private hospitals
Divisional t/o £35m, 110 staff

Financial Accountant - Reporting to Group Financial Accounting Manager
- Prepare monthly finance package using Microcontrol
- Supervise General Ledger, Accounts Payable, and Cashiers functions (4 reports)
- Streamline accounts preparation to achieve strict reporting deadlines focusing on time-critical operations (Lotus 1-2-3)
- Reorganise accounts to facilitate greater line management control and significant tax savings

VIDEO CORP OF LONDON   **1994 – 1998**
Producer/distributor of Arts/Ballet/Opera films for TV and Video
T/o £12m, 25 staff

Production Accountant - Reporting to Financial Controller
- Financial accounting for several film company subsidiaries
- Production accounting – point of contact for Production/Sales staff
- Project appraisal – production budgets and cash flows. Co-producer/royalty reporting
- Devised & introduced new Union Production Agreement with MU/Equity ensuring continuation of UK productions while making considerable 'up-front' cost reductions
- Cultivated good relations with MU/Equity
- Simplified and standardised royalty accounting and reporting

SPORT WORLD   **1992 – 1994**
New York Times publishing company

Accountant - Reporting to Company Secretary
- Day-to-day accounting with two staff
- Monthly and statutory accounts
- Computerisation study, identifying potential solutions and setting specification. Implementing preferred solution.

Page 1 of 2

BAYWATER plc   1989 – 1992
Toy importers and electrical wholesalers

Assistant to Group Finance Director
- Involved in consolidations and treasury Head Office roles
- Accountancy support for subsidiaries – monthly management accounts/budgets/cash flows plus supervisory support for each location's accounts staff

BUCKMASTER   1984 – 1988
Specialist printers and publishers

Financial and Management Accounts Clerk
Monthly accounts, reconciliations, stock evaluations

JAB BEALES   1981 – 1984
Chartered Accountants

Accounts Clerk
Incomplete records and personal tax

QUALIFICATION AND TRAINING

ACCA   1997
ACCA   CPE courses
Various computer skills courses

PERSONAL

Dob 23.06.64
Married, two children (13 and 10)

Commentary

Rod is a good mid-range accountant or smaller company senior finance man. The CV talks to his general accounting experience across a number of sectors – which matches up well with the profile. Rod found it hard to identify and quantify key achievements, so he has focussed on the responsibilities.

CV 6 – IT manager's CV

Brett Hollows

17 Devonshire Street, Norwich, Norfolk NR2 4JB
Tel: 01603 456 987 Mob: 07802 648 345
Email: bretthollows@lineone.net

Customer-focussed IT professional, with 15 years' experience in finance and manufacturing environments. Good communication skills, at all levels, to support customers through all stages from problem identification to system implementation. Good team management skills.

Key skills:

- Defining and analysing business requirements, setting out tender requests, and reviewing tenders
- Managing projects to timely completion on cost, either through a team or through own efforts
- Up-to-date with current technology (software and hardware)
- Experience with a wide range of software and platforms

EMPLOYMENT SUMMARY

TRILOGY FINANCE PLC   2002 – 2005
Systems Consultant

Part of team revising and replacing key financial systems. Advised especially on use of J D Edwards systems.

- Planned and managed transition of financial systems from J D Edwards to Oracle, meeting   budget timescales
- Selected suppliers, managed and trained as required to transfer four major outsourcing projects without downtime
- Specified and implemented new SAP systems, following specific SAP training programme

UNITY MANUFACTURING   1995 – 2002
IT Manager

Responsible for operations and management of IT department (15) and all IT operations.

- Managed major group and local projects on AS400s, delivering planned results on time
- Led development of projects to implement J D Edwards systems modules, through complete project cycle to meet business requirements
- Successfully implemented, supported and maintained new payroll systems for group
- Developed first corporate web-site, specifying need, recruiting necessary new team, managing development and implementation. Initiated regular update timetable with other departments

LUXFIELD GROUP   1993 – 1995
Business Analyst

Responsible for project management and support of all finance and supply chain management systems

- Developed strategy for migrating from existing platforms to AS400s, involving assessment of corporate needs, gaining sign-off, preparing RTT, selecting preferred supplier and overseeing introduction
- Developed management experience by running team projects – successfully

SUTTON & McCARTHY plc   1990 – 1993
Senior Analyst/Programmer

Covering a wide variety of systems projects from project specification, through package selection, analysis, testing, support and implementation for Hoskyns Insight Accounts.

PRIOR EXPERIENCE   1984 – 1990

Various roles from trainee programmer to senior programmer in temporary and freelance roles, working on mainframes and AS400s.

QUALIFICATIONS AND TRAINING

1984 B Sc (Hons) Maths and Computing – University of South Bank
1983 3 'A' levels
1981 7 GCSEs

TECHNICAL TRAINING

Wide range of courses to develop and maintain leading edge in J D Edwards, Oracle, and SAP systems. Other training includes LSDM, Project Management, Showcase, Business Objects, Lotus Notes, RPG and Synon.

PERSONAL DETAILS

Dob 22.03.64
Married, four children (13, 12, and 10 and 7)
Interest: Real tennis and Formula 1

Commentary

Brett has moved from programming to managing an IT department, so he has not spelled out his early experience as a programmer. Rather than list out all the courses he has attended, he has summarised them under the type of software covered.

CV 7 – A recent graduate's CV

EVIE GOODMAN BSc (HONS)

THE COTTAGE • MONKS ROAD • BROMLEY • KENT • BR3 5SL
Phone 07853 608580 • E-mail eviegoodman@hotmail.com

EXAM RESULTS

Royal Holloway College, University of London	2001-2004
BSc Hons (2.1) Mathematics with statistics	
Bromley High School, GDST	1987-2001

A Levels - Mathematics Grade B, English Grade B, Biology Grade C

During my first year at sixth form, I studied independently at home due to illness. This involved working through the syllabuses using text books and study guides. Through this I achieved the ability to work confidently on my own, developed great self motivation, and excellent organisational skills.

GCSEs - 2A*s, 6As and 2Bs

WORK EXPERIENCE

J Coral - Betting assistant   06/03 – date
Taking bets, using a touch screen computer, and giving out winnings. Handling large sums of money in a busy environment.

Andrew Jones Estate Agent   06/03 – date
Administrative work including writing, sending out letters and filing.

McCarthy and Shaw – Solicitors   04/03 – 06/03
Undertook work experience looking at employment and property cases.

Pavilion Leisure Centre - Crèche helper   09/02 - 04/03
Working with another member of staff supervising children from 6 months - 5 years with reading and colouring. Helping with the business side by filling out registration forms. Prioritising jobs in a busy environment was very important.

Pavilion Leisure Centre - Children's party organiser   08/02 - 11/02
Solely responsible for organising games and tea for between 10 - 20 children from 5 - 11 years. Effective communication and leadership skills were important.

Pavilion Leisure Centre - Summer camp leader   07/02 - 09/02
Organised games and supervised swimming sessions, trips, and lunch for up to 50 children. Communication, patience and thinking on one's feet were very important skills needed.

Cazenove and Co. - Stockbrokers   06/99
Took the place of an employee who was off sick. Handling the "back office" paper work for the transactions in the International Department.

VOLUNTEER EXPERIENCE

Helping at the Sunday School at St. George's Church, Beckenham supervising singing, reading the bible and painting.

Whilst undertaking the role as charity representative, helped organise a karaoke and a fashion show generating £1000.

At University, helping with the departmental interview days. Carrying out tours of the campus and answering questions from the prospective undergraduates and their parents

INTERESTS AND ACTIVITIES

Sport - playing tennis at Hayes Tennis Club and at university. Attending Shotokan Karate twice a week at The Knight's Club in Bromley where I have recently been awarded my 5th Kyu. A keen swimmer competing regularly at school and county level, and for a swimming club in individual and team events. Playing the piano since the age of five reaching Grade 6 standard.

IT SKILLS

Certificate of Competence in Information Technology, Microsoft Word/Excel. University using basic Mathematica (pure mathematics), Minitab (statistics) and Microsoft Outlook. At Andrew Jones Estate Agent using Propco.

PERSONAL INFORMATION

- Date of Birth: 17/08/83
- Full Driving Licence

Commentary

Notice how Evie, who has only recently left university, has brought in various voluntary and part-time roles to 'fill out' the career section of her CV. She explains the unusual circumstances while taking her A-levels, without making excuses for grades that were below her expectations.

CV 8 – An interim manager's CV

John Peabody
Outsourcing Consultant & Interim Mgr

Key Skills:

- **Outsourcing Process & Implementation**
  - Well versed in all aspects of the outsourcing process from initial scope definition through vendor appraisal to ongoing vendor management. Considerable 'hands on' experience across a wide variety of outsourcing projects - $10m to $200m at local and international level.
- **Procurement & Contract Management**
  - Considerable experience in all aspects of procurement & contract management, from initial vendor selection through contract negotiation to ongoing partner relationship management. Vendor experience includes IBM; EDS; SAIC; Sema; Logica; Scicon; P&O Road Transport.
- **Project, Change, & Implementation Management**
  - Extensive experience in the processes and skills required to manage and implement business change and other major projects, e.g. global ERP implementation & support; major merger & acquisition; establishment of new commercial, procurement and logistics departments.

Career   **Period**

- **Independent Consultant**   2004 - 2005
  - Worked with Metra Consulting in a major bid preparation for the Worcester Police Service.
  - Worked with a major printer in a bid preparation for XYZ (GB), won contract
  - Evaluated SMARTSOURCING, and participated in outsourcing forum reviews for Supply Management magazine.
- **Employment**
  - **ABC Chemicals**   1978 - 2004
    Contracts Mgr; Outsourcing Transition / Project Mgr; Commercial Mgr; ERP Systems Mgr; Materials Mgr; Distribution & Warehousing Mgr;
  - **Bishops**   1973 - 1978
    IT Systems Mgr; Sales Planning Mgr; Purchasing Mgr
  - **British Leyland**
    Castings buyer (from graduate entry) 1968-1973

Personal Information & Contact details:

  - Calm logical professional with strong interpersonal and communication skills, with a positive 'get things done' attitude. Extensive European and International experience.
  - BSc Econ (Hons); CIPS; Project Management Certified
  - Languages English, with some French & German

John Peabody
98 The Cutting, Haywards Heath, RH16 1AB Tel: 01444 456789 Mobile 07777 234567
Email: johnpeabody@peabody.co.uk

Page 1 of 2

Recent Projects:

Date	Project
2004 - date	Worked with a major outsourcing consultancy preparing bid for Police. Re-tendering Outsourcing and Procurement Optimisation project. Evaluated, bid and won major contract with XYZ (GB) Evaluated SMARTSOURCING, and participated in outsourcing review forums for Supply Management magazine
2000- 2004	Successfully managed $200m IT Contract for delivery of Applications & Host support to 20 locations across Europe & USA. Spent 2 weeks / mth in the USA for 18 mths. Part of the team which negotiated the IBM Contract saving circa 10% costs, while stabilising the support services Chemicals DB representative on ABC Group project to optimise DB procurement and implement e- procurement tools.
1999- 2000	Part of the Chemicals IT team which successfully integrated United Chemicals into ABC (worked on the merger pre announcement)
1994- 2000	Successfully transitioned various UK, European & US locations to ABC's major IT outsource partners.(IBM; EDS; SAIC) Directly involved in all aspects of the outsourcing process from initial scope definition through RFP Vendor selection, to Contract negotiation and start up. Key interface between IT Vendor and the Business Mgrs
1990- 1994	Successfully managed the support, training, and further roll out of Chemicals ERP system to USA & Asia Pacific, to 1500 users. Outsourced the CS applications support team to Logica Spent 12 mths located in Antwerp, Belgium, establishing a stand alone Commercial Dept
1988- 1990	Worked with the team that developed the initial functional definition, and acceptance testing of the Chemicals ERP system, then successfully managed the roll out of the Chemicals ERP system, across 14 UK & European locations, spending 6/8 weeks at each location
1981- 1988	Managed the supply chain systems & function for 650 ktpa, across 3 separate production locations. Part of the team which successfully integrated Pride into ABC (within 6 weeks)
1978- 1981	Outsourced the bulk road tanker fleet to P& O Transport, saving circa 30% costs without service disruption.
1976- 1978	Implemented a mini computer system to run the ERP activities across 3 UK locations. and improved the overall accuracy of the stock control & order processing systems.
1975- 1976	Worked on the sales product range optimisation
1973- 1975	Established a new Purchasing Dept, and integrated it into both the European & International US Purchasing functions
1968- 1973	Joined as a Commercial Graduate, and then moved through PA to Director of Purchasing, to front line procurement with National Bus, and AEC Motors. Involved in implementing a Ford style procurement function.

Commentary (see page 119, after the following CV)

CV 9 – An academic CV

Name: Michael John Seymour
Current position: Professor of Psychology
Department: Psychology
Faculty: Science

Educational qualifications (tertiary)
1980   PhD Kings College London University UK
1976   MSc Psychology Bristol University UK
1975   BSc(Hons) Psychology, Durham University UK

Previous appointments
1997-   Professor in Psychology, University of Leeds
1989-97   Associate Professor in Psychology, University of Leeds
1982-9   Senior Lecturer in Psychology, University of Leeds
1980   Lecturer in Psychology, Kings College London UK

Significant awards and distinctions
1980   Bowman Scholarship to Kings College
[details of committee memberships, chairmanships of committees, fellowships, nominations for awards (even if not successful), directorships etc. All with dates]

Professional societies etc

[Memberships of relevant societies, special positions with groups/ divisions/ societies etc.
Memberships of any editorial boards, representation on review bodies for significant professional magazines/journals
Assessment of any grant applications (for independent funding bodies)
All with dates]

Invited seminars, talks, and conferences

[Listing of key seminars, talks and conferences presented with dates, possibly analysed national/international to aid reader. Speaker/presenter, chair/facilitator, etc]

Internal committees and teaching posts

[Listing of such positions with dates]

Research specialities

[Details of specialities, key national/international recognition, with dates.
Supervision of PhDs, Masters degree students etc.]

Publications

[Listing of books published by category with dates of publication
Listing of chapters in books, videos etc
Listing of all peer-reviewed/refereed journal articles (relevant journals) with dates (in preparation, submitted, reviewed, and published) e.g.:
2004   Seymour MJ, Mathewson JP, Eidelberg JS [Title as in publication], [Journal title], [Number], [Pages]
         The order of the names should be as in the relevant journal]

Page 1 of ** - Michael Seymour

Grants and funding obtained

[Listing of grants obtained with details of funding body, amount and dates]

Page * of ** - Michael Seymour

Commentary

This CV is based on a 'real' academic CV promoted by the university as its 'house style' – I have excluded all the detail in the interests of brevity, but you should list all significant items under each section – making perhaps 6+ pages in all

Commentary
(on John Peabody's CV shown on pages 116/117)

John was a senior manager working for a very large company who decided he wanted to take on interim work. His CV has been crafted to show the projects he managed within his employment, (i.e. in a similar manner to interim projects) rather than putting them as achievements within a job. Indeed, some aspects of the job are omitted.

119

APPENDIX II

Words and phrases it may be better to avoid!

I started writing down a few words or phrases that often irritate readers when they appear in CVs – whether professional recruiters, recruiting managers or even coaches. The list grew as I talked to more people, most of whom also had their own pet hates. What I have set out here is a general list of avoidable words – some of which you might never even think of using. Many should be avoided in your CV and in any letters you write – and the rest probably should be avoided in conversations, interviews and so on.

Sometimes a cliché is needed and some of these words can be used on some occasions – as long as they are not over-used. It also depends on context and sometimes it may be appropriate to use a word to add zest, imagination and interest to your story – but beware of business-speak! Probably the best motto is to try to keep it simple and 'Queen's English'.

If there is a better, clearer, or shorter way of saying it, use it!

24/7
Absolutely
Acronyms (excessive use of e.g. KPIs, HR, NIH, CFO, CEO, MD,....)
Actually (at the start of every phrase)
Address the issue
After consultation with my colleagues
All-singing, all-dancing
All things considered
At the end of the day
At this moment in time
Ballpark figure
Bandwidth (as in 'I don't have the bandwidth to consider that')
Basically
Bear with me
Between a rock and a hard place
Big picture

Blue sky thinking
Bread and butter
Clearly...
Crack troops
Draw a line under
Epicentre
Face time
Finger on the pulse
Firm but fair (as in 'my management style is ...')
First base
Game plan
Going forward
Heads up (e.g. I'll give you a heads up on that.)
I hear what you say
I'm bound to say
Innit?
In the final analysis
Leverage
Like (when used at the start of a sentence and especially every other
    word!)
Literally
Low hanging fruit
Metrics (as in 'get the metrics on this..')
Mission critical
Mission statement
Movers and shakers
My understanding is...
No-brainer
No two ways about it
Obviously
Paradigm shift
Personally
Proactive
Pushing the envelope
Quality time
Quite frankly
Radar (on the, above the, below the)

Rainmaker

Respectfully (as in 'respectfully ask you')

Scenario

Sharing (as in 'let me share this with you')

Showstopper

Singing from the same hymn-sheet

Striking the right balance.

Talk with (instead of 'talk to') unless you are American

Team player

The fact of the matter is

The view from 10,000 feet

Thinking outside the box

Ticks in boxes

To be honest/frank/candid

Touch base

Triage (when used in business – perfectly OK in medical situations)

Up to speed

Value added

Very very

Well (at the start of every sentence)

Window of opportunity

With due respect

With all due respect

You know what I mean?

Index